Praise for *R*

"Georgina Cannon's *Return Again* is a very powerful tool and important for anyone wanting to better understand themselves."

— Brit Elders, CEO of *www.ShirleyMacLaine.com*

"Georgina is so knowledgeable about the subject of past lives and interlives. Her writing style is a pleasure to read and easy to understand if you're not familiar with the subject matter. Can highly recommend the latest book!"

— Hannah Murray, presenter and producer, Talk Radio Europe

"Georgina Cannon's *Return Again* gives proof that we are eternal beings who have come to this life to learn lessons and evolve spiritually. Georgina, herself a master hypnotherapist, shows through powerful anecdotes and profoundly well-researched documentation that past lives and inter-lives are real, and not just for the few believers, but for anyone willing to discover who they really are."

— Darlene Montgomery, author of *Dream Yourself Awake* and *Conscious Women, Conscious Lives*

"The world *is* ready for *Return Again*! Georgina's passion and expertise teach us once and for all that we are *not* our bodies. She reminds us that what we don't overcome in this lifetime, we must do in the next. A thoughtful, inspiring and motivating read for anyone looking to get the most out of *this* lifetime!

"An empowering book teaching us that *we* are in charge of our destiny and that by acknowledging past life experiences and releasing past life fears, we are more free to experience pure joy in the here and now."

"*Return Again* and Georgina's work is brilliant and relevant! No matter what challenges we are faced with in this lifetime, whether it be physical pain, illness, fear, addiction, or depression, she teaches us that we can overcome anything once we understand the root of where the negative patterns have begun: in our past lives."

—Jay Bradley, host of *Live, Look, Feel* (*www.livelookfeel. wordpress.com*), lifestyle coach, and author

"At long last Dr. Cannon has delivered to us the amazing, eloquent and soulfully attuned written work *Return Again: How to Find Meaning in Your Past Lives and Your Interlives*. This book will uplift your mind, body, heart and soul as you weave your way through these exquisite translations that shed new meanings and bring forth new light on soul agreements, karmic interweaves, deja vu and how we can find and meet our perfectly aligned soul mate. A joy to drink from the well of wisdom and inspiration."

—Dr. Ronald A. Alexander, author of *Wise Mind, Open Mind: finding Purpose and Meaning in Times of Crisis, Loss and Change*, Executive Director of the Open Mind Training Institute, Santa Monica, CA

Return
Again

Return Again

How to Find Meaning in Your Past Lives and Your Interlives

Georgina Cannon

San Francisco, CA / Newburyport, MA

First published in 2012 by Weiser Books
Red Wheel/Weiser, LLC
With offices at:
665 Third Street, Suite 400
San Francisco, CA 94107
www.redwheelweiser.com

Copyright © 2012 by Dr. Georgina Cannon

ISBN: 978-1-57863-528-3

Library of Congress Cataloging-in-Publication Data available upon request

Cover design by Barbara Fisher/www.levanfisherdesign.com
Cover photo © Triff /shutterstock
Interior by Dutton & Sherman
Typeset in Didot and Futura

Printed in the United States of America
MAL

10 9 8 7 6 5 4 3 2 1

The paper used in this publication meets the minimum requirements of the American National Standard for Information Sciences—Permanence of Paper for Printed Library Materials Z39.48-1992 (R1997).

To my aunt, Rachel Lewis, who lived a full creative life and taught me to always reach for the stars. Her voice is with me.

It's over—again—for a while
Time to revisit
whatever's been and been seen.
You return once more
To peace, a timeless place
in a placeless time.
Soul space,
of quietude and wonder,
of wisdom and learning.
Until next time.
The trepidation of a new beginning
the anticipation of a new threshold
the joy of feeling without thought
discovering the world again.
Color, depth, and harmonies,
feet on the earth,
heart in your hands.
Exploring,
the pure happiness of time,
to be, to create, to watch,
to do or do nothing,
running or standing still.
Time for you
and a new sunrise on your soul.

—Georgina Cannon

Contents

and that both mother and baby remain together for the journey through the chosen lifetime. But it isn't always that way.

According to ancient teachings, there are seven planes of existence: the material plane, the one we identify as our physical world; the force plane, or etheric plane; the astral plane; and the mental plane. Very little is known about the three planes that follow these except that they are believed to be of a high degree of spiritual evolution.

Many people seem unaware that their souls are on a journey. The levels we attain, therefore, show us where we currently are and how far we have yet to journey. As I tell my clients: If you don't get it right in this lifetime, you'll have to come back and repeat the same lesson again! This is the concept of karma, the Hindu and Buddhist idea that what goes around comes around, the cornerstone of reincarnation. Through rebirth we achieve enlightenment—the ability to love perfectly and have true inner peace.

In our culture, we have learned to fear death as the cessation of life, the end of pleasure, of experience, of all that we know on this earth. Because it represents the end of everything, death is often seen by those who suffer unbearable pain or anguish as a release or an escape from their suffering. For others, however, death is not an end, nor is life just a beating heart and measurable brainwave activity. It is a training ground in which we learn the art of dying so that we can live again. For these people, life never dies.

Have you ever met anyone that you seem to know a lot about, even though you've never met them before? A new brother-in-law? Your child's teacher? Are you drawn to visit or live in a place you've never seen? Spain? Kenya? Are there other periods of history that you feel you're aligned with—the Crusades or the French Revolution—even though you have no apparent connection to them? Then you've quite possibly experienced these phenomena in another lifetime. We can discover why we choose the lives we choose through past-life regression.

When most people think of soul mates, they think in terms of "forever," "life partner," and "two halves of one whole." People think of a soul mate as their one and only true love. However, meeting your soul mate is not always synonymous with meeting your life partner or lover. Soul-mate relationships are not necessarily romantic relationships, and you almost always have more than one. These soul mates are considered by many to be part of your soul circle or soul group. And your soul circles travel together with you through many lifetimes, under the terms of carefully negotiated soul contracts.

If you believe in reincarnation in nature—like the seed of a plant recycling through the seasons—then you believe that it could possibly also be so with us—that the seed of who you are leaves one body and returns in another. Think of it as one door opening and another closing—but what about the corridor between the doors? What about the time between these incarnated lifetimes? We enter a place that the *Tibetan Book of the Dead* calls Bardo—or the Interlife, or the Labyrinth, or the Blue Mist of Life Between Lives—where the goal is to remember who we truly are at the level of pure spirit and soul. To look and consider the past and to plan for learning in our future—the body we choose, the life we live, and what karma we bring with us.

Hell on earth is a given right now. Practically everywhere you look, you can see evidence of the ghastly state into which so much of the world has fallen. And so it has been for a while, as seen in Dante's timeless Inferno. Heaven on earth is also a given right now. The blossoming of trees and flowers each spring. The giggle of little girls. A crying, ongoing belly laugh with my sister and friends. The purr of a cat on a lap, or the wet nose of a dog in the hand. I have often wondered if, in fact, our Interlives, as our heaven and hell, are right here, right now, at this time, on this planet. Moreover, we can choose heaven over hell using simple techniques.

Preface

The study and experience of regression journeys is a personal one, and can only be received as such.

Although the research by this and other authors is extensive, it does not replace the wisdom and experience of each and every personal journey taken by the reader.

The reader (not the author) assumes full responsibility for his or her own journey through this and other regression experiences, for all the consequences of any and all mental or physical activity undertaken as a result of reading this book or in attempting to apply, in any way, anything discussed or described herein.

This book is not intended to replace the need for medical or other appropriate therapeutic assistance. The author urges the reader to obtain assistance and advice from an appropriately qualified person prior to attempting to apply, in any way, anything discussed or described in this book.

Acknowledgments

First, I must acknowledge the guidance of the late Henry Bolduc, who not only introduced me to the power of facilitating past-life regression, but also demonstrated how to teach it by putting aside the self. This lesson has served me well in lecturing, teaching, and working with clients.

Next, I want to thank the audiences, the thousands of clients, and graduate students from whom, over the years, I have received both awe and humility in sharing their extraordinary soul journeys. They help spread the word and healing, helping one person at a time to recognize their own magnificence.

I honor and pay homage to researchers and practitioners who have gone before me: Edgar Cayce, Dolores Cannon, Roger Woolger, Joel Whitton, Ormond McGill, and Michael Newton, whose vocation has been the foundation and touchstone for my work with clients and students for the past years.

Finally, grateful thanks to Penny Hozy, always, and my agent, Devra Ann Jacobs, whose faith in my work helped through the rewrite times to achieve excellence and clarity. This couldn't have happened without your support. I am grateful.

Namaste.

This book is a compilation of learned, intuitive, channeled, and experienced information. It is one person's point of view—with the additional help of the teachers and writers quoted herein.

Please enjoy this book with an appreciation of what it can give you—take what works for you now, and leave the rest for another time—or never.

As with all teaching, I believe there is more than one source, and I encourage you to keep reading, researching, discovering, and playing your way toward understanding and peace in this lifetime and discovering your magnificence.

Namaste.

Introduction

Alice laughed. "There's no use trying," she said, "one can't believe impossible things."

"I daresay you haven't had much practice," said the Queen. "When I was your age, I always did it for half-an-hour a day. Why, sometimes I've believed as many as six impossible things before breakfast."

— Lewis Carroll

It was the headaches that did it. Blinding, seemingly everlasting migraine headaches that took days and joy out of my life. I had tried everything to alleviate the cell-vibrating throbbing that started with a zazzy aura at the outer fringes of my vision, and focused a short time later behind my left eye and through the left side of my head. Agony. Nothing seemed to help. Allopathic, homeopathic, naturopathic—I tried them all, including an expensive series of sessions with an international "healer" who claimed to heal all ills.

By this time, I had started a hypnosis school and clinic in Toronto and had worked with various hypnotists at the clinic, using pain-management hypnosis. It didn't work. Then someone recommended hypnotic regression—back to the cause—the theory being that all pain has an emotional root, and that all you have to do is find that root.

As fate—or karma—would have it, I had signed up to learn the official protocols to run past-life regression sessions—always believing that we are more than we seem.

Coming from England, I believed there were fairies at the bottom of the garden and that ghosts existed—and if they existed, they were the soul, somewhere—and I wanted to find out where that somewhere was, and how it worked.

Knowing that the training included practice sessions, I decided, what the heck, I'll try it. I would have tried anything to get rid of the migraines at that point! But back to cause . . . hmmm . . . could they have come from the repeated head-bashing I received from my mother as a child? (They came with the precursor of her going around the house, closing all the windows so the neighbors wouldn't hear, then grabbing me by my hair and bashing the back of my head against the wall while she screamed the list of my misdemeanors.) But I'd worked through that with years of therapy—so it couldn't be that. Or maybe it was the time I slipped at the swimming pool and crashed my head against the diving board. Hmm . . . I'd forgotten about that. Well, one way to find out!

As we paired up for practice, my partner agreed to see if we could discover the root of my migraines. "Sure," he said, "we can try." To be honest, neither of us was that confident in the process yet—and this added another layer of uncertainty!

Relaxed in the chair, I heard the trainee past-life facilitator's voice leading me back through time and space, and suddenly an awful stench surrounded me. It was disgusting. Putrid. I felt like vomiting—and then I realized it was coming from me. I stank!

I suddenly saw and knew myself as a decrepit hag with rotting teeth and filthy, lank strings of hair. It was hard to see my skin color it was so encrusted with dirt. I found myself living in a cave just outside a small Mediterranean village, and I knew immediately what my role was. I birthed babies in the village and gathered herbs for abortions and easier births. I was the desired and reviled "witch" the villagers called on in times of trouble. And then chased away or, at best, ignored.

I was paid with food, when they remembered—and most of the time they didn't, or chose not to. I was always close to starvation, especially in the winter. But the birthing of babies and the brief, grateful acknowledgements I received from the women when they needed my help kept me going.

Depleted and exhausted, I had just returned from a difficult birth. The baby—a boy—came feet first with the cord around his neck, and he was dead. I had cleaned up the mother and stopped the bleeding, given the body of the child to women relatives, and dragged myself back to my cave. And slept.

I woke to the sounds of shouting and heavy footsteps in my cave. A man was standing above me holding a rock. He started to beat me with the rock, blaming me for the death of his son and his wife, who had subsequently died. He kicked me and screamed at me, his spittle spraying my skin.

Suddenly, the rock came down on my eye, into my brain—and then, blackness.

The facilitator guided me through the soul's leaving the body and looking down at the scene below. The husband had killed me with the rock, through my left eye and into the left side of my brain. We completed the protocol of healing, forgiveness, and wisdom, and I returned to this lifetime, shaken and in awe of the process. Maybe that was it! Not the head beating, or the swimming-pool accident, but this past life.

Time would prove if it had worked. I waited for the next migraine to come. More than a decade later, I'm still waiting!

This was the start of my journey of studying, learning, teaching, writing, and appearing in and on the media as a spokesperson for the power of regression therapy—both past-life and Interlife.

This book is designed to hold your hand along the path toward the awe-inspiring possibilities that can enrich your current life. Because, ultimately, it is this current life that is the most important—and everything we do, I believe, needs to be focused on improving who we are, and where we are now.

Chapter 1

Your Body

*Man has no Body distinct from his Soul; for that called
Body is a portion of Soul discerned by the five Senses, the
chief inlets of Soul in this age.*

— WILLIAM BLAKE

Most of us aren't aware of how extraordinary the body is. We
only know it's too fat or too thin, too wide or too short. We
don't celebrate the brilliant mechanics of the machinery that
houses our essence. By and large, we have one of what we
need (heart, mouth, thymus gland) or two of what we need
(kidneys, lungs, eyes), and, most of the time, they all work
well together. Without any conscious thought, we go about
our days—walking, talking, making decisions, eating, loving,
acting, and reacting—and yet not once do we stop and say:
"Wow, this body thing I have is really amazing!" But when
we do take the time to look at this structure, we discover how
truly extraordinary it is.

During our lives on this planet, 500,000 body cells die each second. Each day, about 50 billion cells in our bodies are replaced, resulting in a completely new body each year.

Every year, about 98 percent of the molecules and atoms in our bodies are replaced. Each living being is in an unstable balance of two opposing processes of continual disintegration and integration. We don't appreciate this constant change or its possible impact on our lives. But where does the continuity of our continually changing bodies come from? We know that cells are just the building blocks of the body—like the bricks of a house—but who is the architect; who is the engineer who coordinates the building of this house?

When someone dies, only mortal remains are left. But where is the director of the body? What about consciousness when we die? Is "someone" the body?

Do We "Have" a Body?

The belief is, in essence, that everything and everyone is part of a pattern and thus interconnected. And we connect and interconnect with each other through an altered state or transcendent state of consciousness.

This state allows us to "plug into" the earth and universal energies to heal ourselves and others, both directly and across boundaries. This state also allows us to access our "guides," or spirit helpers, to heal or balance our energy aura or chakras.

The medium—or energy—of this state can be achieved through hypnosis, meditation, or prayer. Many who follow the traditional religions of Christianity, Judaism, or Islam also believe "beyond the book." They believe in a state we call energy, "the light," "the Christ consciousness," *chi*, or "the force."

The idea of past-life regression journeys isn't the shocker it once was. More and more people are recognizing that there is something beyond who we are today, right here, on this planet. And that we are truly the sum of our parts.

And whether the sum of our parts is made up of soul parts or DNA parts, we are more than either, or both, of these.

So, like all curious travelers who wish to explore new, uncharted territory, we can experience surprise, wisdom, occasional discomfort, awe, and delight from the voyage of our souls into the Interlife. Unlike earthly travelers, however, you are unlikely to get tummy troubles on this journey—but then, you don't get air miles either!

Were it not a fact of experience that supreme values reside in the soul . . . psychology would not interest me in the least, for the soul would then be nothing but a miserable vapor.
— CARL JUNG, PSYCHOLOGY AND ALCHEMY

Consider This:

- Do you feel you belong to your body, or does your body belong to you?

- Why do you think you chose the particular body you now inhabit?

- How does your present body serve your purpose?

Chapter 2

The Soul/Body Agreement

*Good for the body is the work of the body, good for the
soul the work of the soul, and good for either the work of
the other.*

— HENRY DAVID THOREAU

We generally assume that, when a woman becomes pregnant,
most of the time the baby is born complete with a soul, and
that both mother and baby remain together for the journey
through the chosen lifetime.

But it isn't always that way, as my colleagues and I have
learned working with new mothers and mothers-to-be in my
hypnosis clinic.

Sometimes, the soul doesn't enter until after the child is
born—occasionally as long as a few months after.

Sometimes the soul leaves after the start of the forming
of the body and a miscarriage occurs; sometimes the soul
chooses a body that it knows will be aborted; and sometimes
the soul makes the choice of leaving just before birth, or just

after, as in the case of SIDS (Sudden Infant Death Syndrome). In those cases, the baby dies before it lives the life the parent expects.

How and why are these choices made? We know that they are usually grief-ridden for the parents, whenever and however the choice is made—but what could possibly be the reason for such a choice to be made by the soul?

Generally speaking, the soul doesn't actually join the body until the twelfth or thirteenth week after conception—but there are exceptions to this.

Sometimes, a soul is so eager to come in that it joins the mother at the time of conception. Sometimes, the soul is so reticent that it doesn't join the baby until birth or after. The joining of the spiritual and physical is usually harmonious, but occasionally it can be tumultuous. Again, why should this be?

Palden Jenkins says, in his online article "Psychic Abortions" (1999):

> No one knows the inner reasons, existing in their own right, which lie behind a soul's decision to be conceived, and to choose a specific set of parents. Therefore a key part of the process is to glean this from the soul itself . . .
>
> Whatever decision is made (and this is open at the beginning of this process), the final decision, methinks, needs to come from the children/souls. It concerns what is the *most realistically manageable and achievable* evolutionary path forward, for them, and for the parents and for other closely involved people, jointly and severally . . . The "abortion" is done by the child itself—usually within three or so days . . .

In my experience, pre-birth and immediately post-birth souls are well capable of making fully aware life-decisions, especially if supported through it. . . but in the end it is the child-souls who choose whether or not to take on the challenges before them.

Consider This:

- When do you believe your soul joined your body?

- Do you feel it made the right choice of body? Why?

Chapter 3

Planes of Existence

From wonder into wonder, existence opens.

—Lao Tzu

According to ancient teachings, there are seven planes of existence. The first plane is the material plane, the one we identify as our physical world. The second is the force plane, or etheric plane. Then comes the astral plane, followed by the mental plane. Very little is known about the three planes that follow these, except that they are believed to be of a high degree of spiritual evolution.

New writings and ideas continue to come forward about spiritual evolution and understanding. Jim Self, in his book *The Shift* (2009)—as well as on his website, *masteringalchemy. com*—talks about a shift of time and consciousness awareness, and how two massive waves of light and energy are moving through this universe and this earth planet, taking us to a heightened sense of awareness and consciousness. As we move into an awareness—even subconsciously—of the next wave or two of energy, and into more awareness of the now, we need to let go of past remembered hurts and move strongly into the now. That means letting go of just responding to noise, motion, action, and reaction, and moving into a time of choice. We will choose how we want to live, react, think, and feel in each now. Without judgment—right or wrong, good or bad—or fear of punishment.

According to Jim Self, we are moving more toward an awareness of being and living as the souls that we truly are!

When a person dies, his or her spirit and astral body go to one of the sub-planes of the astral world, where the spirit rests in a peaceful and regenerative sleep. During this sleep, it undergoes a cleansing and prepares for whatever place corresponds to its level of spiritual development. The astral body remains in the astral world for a brief time after the spirit leaves it. When the spirit awakens, it passes to the mental plane, from where it proceeds to its appropriate level. In *The Beginner's Guide for the Recently Deceased* (2004), David Staume says:

> You probably noticed, soon after the death of your body, that you hadn't gone anywhere in space—you were pretty much in the room you died in, or around about the bus that hit you . . . all that actually occurred was that your consciousness changed focus. You were no longer focused in your physical body—you were focused in the body you have now. It's called your astral body, and the world it allows you to perceive is called the astral world.

Eventually, the astral body loses strength and disintegrates like the physical body. The more spiritually advanced a person is, the faster his or her astral body disintegrates.

The Astral World

Migene González-Wippler, in her 1997 book *What Happens after Death: Scientific & Personal Evidence for Survival*, tells us:

> In the astral world there are zones of great beauty and light that are occupied by higher spirits, but there are also places of darkness and terror inhabited by dark and destructive entities. These terrifying habitations have also been created by the mental vibrations and memories of the beings that inhabit them, most of whom committed terrible crimes and other destructive acts during their material lives.

Each plane of existence in the astral world has its own vibratory rate. The higher the plane, the faster its vibratory rate. The vibratory rate of a spirit depends on its evolutionary development; it will be in perfect harmony with the plane to which it belongs. Spirits are not able to ascend to a superior plane, where the vibrations are stronger and faster, but they can descend to a lower plane and remain there for as long as they wish. According to most mystical schools, higher spirits descend to the lower levels of the astral plane to help the spirits who inhabit these darker regions seek redemption.

We enter the astral world, or Interlife, for a period of time in order to rest and learn. This is the time when we evaluate where we have been and where we need to go next. Our actions in the life just past are examined and measured against our karmic destiny. Have we learned the lessons of that destiny or must we repeat them? We don't undertake the journey alone—we are offered assistance in the form of spirit guides, who are able to consult with a council of higher spirits that meets in a council chamber in the center of a powerful energy field. Dolores Cannon describes it this way, in *Between Death and Life: Conversations with a Spirit* (1995):

> If you were to look at it with physical eyes it would appear that where we are gathered is suspended in midair, but it is really not. It is supported by an energy field that you cannot perceive with the eyes of your level. The energy field is a beautiful deep violet color and it surrounds all of us. There are not really any definite walls or ceilings; everything is just this deep violet and gold. And suspended in the center of this energy field is a council chamber, I suppose you would call it.

As we understand it—and Interlife journeys seem to prove it—members of this council have reached a more advanced plane than most, but have not yet attained the highest plane, that of total enlightenment. They work closely with those who guide individuals on the lower planes. These spirit guides see things as they appear on the physical plane, so they can help individuals plan their future paths and make their choices.

In *Between Death and Life*, Cannon goes on to tell us this about the relationship between our decision-making and the role of the council:

You are truly the master of your own fate and destiny. You, yourself are in complete control of what you call your lifetime. You are the one who is making decisions as to when and where and how. We [on the council], from our point of view, can see all the options spread out before you. But it is you, yourself who must make the final decisions. You also cannot help but influence other individuals while you are living on this plane. You influence individuals continuously.

Those on the council switch back and forth between lifetimes, sometimes working on a general council and sometimes acting as guides. Those who are guides have usually served on the general council and there is much interchange of information between the two. This allows for greater awareness as well as different perspectives. I see them as spiritual consultants—soul project managers, in a way.

Before we begin our return trip into the physical life, we go through a series of planning sessions with our guides and teachers. During this process, we also check out the family we are considering joining in our next life on earth. Yes, we choose our parents!

In chapter six of *The Book of the Soul* (2004), Ian Lawton gives us the graphic description of the process of choosing lives during the Interlife, comparing it to being in a theater and watching an interactive movie:

Here souls are able to review the various options available to them in terms of a selection of human beings that will be incarnate with more or less the right sort of aptitudes, circumstances and environment, at about the right time, perhaps in a number of geographic locations. So effectively this place is one where the subject can manipulate time and control the movie telepathically as if it were a video playback, fast-forwarding where necessary and even pausing the scene to enter it temporarily and gain direct experience of that particular incarnation.

Consider This:

- Have you experienced the astral state between the times of sleeping and being awake?

- How did it feel? Did you have any "insights" that you may have put aside since that time? What were they?

- Why do you think you chose the parents you have?

- What did that choice teach you?

Chapter 4

Soul Levels and Karma as We Understand Them

Every moment and every event of every man's life on earth plants something in his soul.

— THOMAS MERTON

Both the *Tibetan Book of the Dead* and the *Egyptian Book of the Dead* suggest that, immediately after death, everyone is able to perceive the "Clear Light." However, some souls may be drawn because of anger, desire, or misused lifetimes to less luminous states. Many people seem unaware that their souls are on a journey. And maybe because of that, the periods between lifetimes are uneven in length — some souls need a longer learning period in the life between lives, while others want or need a speedy reincarnation, as they feel their previous lifetimes weren't complete in some way or another.

Do all souls go to all levels? The honest answer is: I don't know! I have asked this question many times, hoping to receive the answer, but my educated guess has to be this: Not all souls go to all levels. It seems, from the various Interlife journeys I have facilitated, as if, depending on the life lived and the way it was lived, the soul can move up (!) two levels, or sometimes three, between lifetimes. For instance, I have had clients who went directly from the second level to the fifth level. It seemed their souls were on a fast-track journey to total enlightenment. Does it happen often? No. But it has happened.

The levels we attain, therefore, show us where we currently are and how far we have yet to journey. As I tell my clients: If you don't get it right in this lifetime, you'll have to come back and repeat the same lesson again! And, yes, my clients groan, too. But it does make for a stronger focus to try and get things right this time around.

The soul levels as we know them are:

1st level: The Elementals—pure energies—rocks, trees, water, the earth. Life/energy/cellular forms with no individual personality—collective life forms waiting for their time.

2nd level: Elementals who deal with plants, trees, and animals, or the land, sea, and air. Also called dryads, sprites, fairies, leprechauns, devas. They have more mischief than intelligence. They exist in the spirit realm—their souls are working toward perfection, just like ours. After they have learned to take care of nature, they can move up and learn to take care of themselves and each other.

3rd level: Humans who do not have the intelligence to be either good or bad; they just live an existence. Animal group souls are also at the third level.

4th level: Humans who are antisocial, criminals, and murderers.

5th level: Humans on the earth level of day-to-day existence.

6th level: The spirit realm—also some humans who are open and aware.

7th level: The soul schools—where we go in the Interlife.

8th and 9th levels: The Great Masters—avatars, Jesus, the Buddha.

10th level: One again with God.

The Role of Karma

Any discussion of soul levels and the metaphysical process needs also to consider the concept of karma. Karma, loosely defined, is the Hindu and Buddhist idea that what goes around comes around. Put another way, what we send into the universe comes back to us. We reap what we sow; we have to pay the consequences for our actions.

Karma is the cornerstone of reincarnation. The whole point of rebirth is to achieve enlightenment—the ability to love perfectly and have true inner peace. We do this by dealing with karma. Karma makes us responsible for our mistakes and unlearned lessons in this life as well as past lives. It's like a hand of cards that we are dealt and must decide how to play. We can choose to live with open eyes, on the lookout for the lessons karma has in store, ready to recognize and learn them. Or we can blindly stumble through, ignoring the lessons. Our choice. "Karma will be seen," says Ormond McGill, "as not expressing what you are, but what you have done to make you what you are" (*Grieve No More, Beloved: The Book of Delight*, 2003).

Repeated experiences lead to wisdom.

—JOSEPH J. WEED, WISDOM OF THE MYSTIC MASTER

The concept of karma has been adopted by our culture in ways we may not realize. Consider, for example, the twelve-step programs that alcoholics and other addicts embrace to overcome their addictions. At a website called 12Step.org, I found the following program. Some of the steps ask the participant to review (Step 4), recant (Step 5), and repair past hurts to others (Steps 8 and 9).

> **Step 1:** We admitted we were powerless over our addiction—that our lives had become unmanageable
>
> **Step 2:** Came to believe that a Power greater than ourselves could restore us to sanity
>
> **Step 3:** Made a decision to turn our will and our lives over to the care of God as we understood God
>
> **Step 4:** Made a searching and fearless moral inventory of ourselves

Step 5: Admitted to God, to ourselves and to another human being the exact nature of our wrongs

Step 6: Were entirely ready to have God remove all these defects of character

Step 7: Humbly asked God to remove our shortcomings

Step 8: Made a list of all persons we had harmed, and became willing to make amends to them all

Step 9: Made direct amends to such people wherever possible, except when to do so would injure them or others

Step 10: Continued to take personal inventory and when we were wrong promptly admitted it

Step 11: Sought through prayer and meditation to improve our conscious contact with God as we understood God, praying only for knowledge of God's will for us and the power to carry that out

Step 12: Having had a spiritual awakening as the result of these steps, we tried to carry this message to other addicts, and to practice these principles in all our affairs

How Karma Works

To accept the idea that our actions in this life and in past lives can have an effect on us in the future, we have to accept the idea that actions carry energy. Doing good deeds—being friendly, smiling at a stranger—sends out good energy or vibes. Flipping off a slow driver in the passing lane, "tasting" grapes while shopping at the supermarket, spreading gossip — these actions send out bad energy or vibes.

The vibes we send out through our actions don't just float into space and dissolve. They actually affect things. The energy of our actions is as real as a sound wave; we just don't currently have any real way to detect or "hear" it.

This energy can interact with the atmosphere and the matter inside the atmosphere. Proof of this is seen in the research of Masaru Emoto.

The Power of Thoughts

In his book *The Hidden Messages in Water* (2005), Masaru Emoto studies the effect of projected thoughts and emotions on water molecules. His experiments involve observing the molecules in their original state, then doing things like labeling a bottle of water with the words "I love you" or "Thank you," or playing heavy metal music for a bottle of water, or praying beside a water sample. Afterward, Emoto re-observes the molecules, noting any changes that have taken place.

His discoveries are astounding. In every case, the water that is exposed to positive vibrations forms crystals of the most intricate and beautiful design. One sample that was treated with chamomile oil actually made crystals that mimicked the flower's form. Another sample taken from a Japanese dam appeared as a blob in the "before" picture; but after an hour-long prayer practice next to the dam, a new sample revealed molecules that looked like diamond snowflakes and glittered like crystals.

The water exposed to negative vibrations consistently formed no crystals at all and instead became unstructured, chaotic, and dark. Frozen crystals broke in two when Elvis Presley's "Heartbreak Hotel" was played. A water sample labeled with the words "Adolf Hitler" returned no crystals, no snowflakes, no patterns whatsoever—just images of disorganized, frenzied whorls.

By photographing his water samples in the "before" and "after" states, Emoto provided visual proof again and again of two things. Not only do human thoughts and emotions have the ability to radiate out from the body, but these thoughts and emotions also actually manipulate physical reality. This truth has extraordinary implications. Just think about it for a moment . . .

If our thoughts and words can change the structure of water molecules—if labeling a water sample with the words "I hate you" can distort its molecules—what happens when you say those words to another person, especially considering that the human body is 70 percent water? By the same token, what happens when you say the words "I love you"?

The point is simple and profound: intentions have power. Your words, your actions, thoughts, and feelings—everything you say, think, or do—carry with them the energy that created them. Moreover, those intangible vibrations influence the matter around them.

To put all this into a more scientific frame, think back to your high school physical science class and Newton's third law of motion: For every action, there is an equal and opposite reaction. Newton was talking about the interaction of physical objects. But if we consider "action" in a larger sense—the transfer of energy on a physical, mental, or emotional level—then it's a scientific law that what we send out comes back to us, like a boomerang. What we think about—we bring about. Karma is science. As David Staume tells us: "The Law of Equilibrium is the pendulum of the cosmic clock—will pushing the pendulum one way and karma pushing it back, and so the cosmic clock ticks" (*The Beginner's Guide for the Recently Deceased*, 2004).

◆

If you are agreeing with me so far in this book, you already know that you are more than your physical body. This is not a new idea—that the body is merely the housing for something larger called the soul, or spirit, or aura. Some people call this the energy body—the field of energy that surrounds and permeates the physical body at the deepest cellular levels.

The energy body is like the body's memory. Just as the brain records and files events into a memory bank, the energy body does the same, except the memories are stored in the aura of the body and the spaces or fields around every one of its cells and molecules. This field contains and reflects your energy. It surrounds you and carries with you the emotional energy created—every positive and negative internal and external experience. This emotional force impacts the physical body with what we call the mind-body connection. In this way, your experiences are the tapestry of your life—and they become your biology!

Every event, thought, and feeling is imprinted on your energy body, encoding it with information. This information affects the health of the cells, molecules, and atoms of your body structure.

We must always remember, however, that the soul may have seen the learning in a different way—how we handled life, from the soul's perspective, may have been appropriate. Although we can use the stories that come to us through regression and examples, we must always bear in mind that, ultimately, not one of us on this planet at this time really knows it all! So we have to be gentle with our judgments and certainties, and remain aware of our unknowing.

> *Every human being is the author of his own health or disease.*
>
> — THE BUDDHA

This is where karma comes in. We are not born and given life just because . . . There is a greater spiritual purpose. We are all here to achieve enlightenment, the spiritual state of perfect peace and serenity. We incarnate on earth for as many lifetimes as it takes to learn the lessons we need to learn in order to grow into enlightenment.

We are meant to learn certain things in each lifetime. Each of us has a unique set of lessons to learn. If we don't learn these lessons, we take them into the Interlife and into the next lifetime—at which point, they become past-life lessons that we have to try to learn all over again. "To accept the process of reincarnation," Joel Whitton explains in *Life Between Life: Scientific Explorations into the Void Separating One Incarnation from the Next* (1986), "is to accept that only by taking complete responsibility for ourselves can we hope to achieve rapid personal growth through the cycle of successive rebirths."

The Karma Process—The Source of Wisdom

When we think or worry about karma, it's usually about how it relates to our current lifetime. This is the only lifetime that is significant and relevant to most people. And as, hopefully, we learn lessons along the way in this lifetime (otherwise we'd still need to be potty trained!), we experience situations that allow us to learn lessons from each previous lifetime. It is the period between these lifetimes that allows us to decide whether or not we have learned these lessons—or whether we need to experience the opportunity again so that the lesson may be learned.

It is during the interlude between lifetimes that we choose the lessons we want to learn, analyze what went wrong in our last incarnation, and plan for the next lifetime so that we can ensure we have opportunities to settle what needs settling.

Some people refer to this process as the "soul contract." Ian Victor Henderson, author of *Parables of Life! An Awakening Journey*, explains soul contracts in this way:

> Before we ever even enter into any particular life cycle on this planet, there is a process beforehand that will more or less guide you through your entire life . . .
>
> [Just imagine a] whole group of souls planning and preparing, some of which will have experienced many incarnations together. It is a beautiful, meticulously and intricately planned event each and every time a soul desires to reincarnate . . . There are intricate plans made,

and within those plans [as in all good planning sessions,] there are back-up plans created, several, in fact.

The reason we do this is to set up scenarios in which our souls can learn and grow. During the Interlife period, we decide what lessons we need and want to learn. If there are leftover lessons from a previous lifetime that we were unable to learn, we write those into the new soul contract.

That's what we believe karma is: the Universe's teacher, urging us toward the lessons we've chosen. I keep saying that it's like a hand of cards we are dealt. Every moment of life is a card in that hand. In every moment, we have the power to choose how we will play.

Karma means action that causes development and change, and so is close to what we mean by evolution.

—TIBETAN BOOK OF THE DEAD, TRANSLATED BY ROBERT THURMAN

So, if we die, as many do, with the lesson unlearned, those un-played cards—the unlearned karmic lessons—go with us, encoded into our energy. We carry them into every lifetime until the lifetime when we actually learn the lesson. We are meant to achieve the tenth soul level—to be at one in God's light—and we keep getting cosmic do-overs until we do.

Karma and the Buddha's Noble Truths

The first of the Buddha's Noble Truths is the full understanding of suffering. This goes beyond the recognition of suffering into the subtleties beyond the immediate. When we remove the cause of the suffering, which is the recognition of the state that we call suffering, then we can move beyond the state of suffering into recognition and understanding. Understanding allows for change of circumstance and interpretation. It makes room for action and change. In other words, we see what we are looking for.

The Buddha's Second Noble Truth says that karma is the root cause of suffering.

What! So you're telling me that my suffering is my own fault?

Well, sort of.

It's true. Your own actions do produce your karma, and your karma can produce your suffering. As we discussed earlier, you can choose to focus on the suffering and feel as if you're being punished. Or you can choose to focus on the lesson to be learned.

Hidden in this choice of focus is a magnificent opportunity for release and growth.

> *Pain is inevitable. Suffering is optional.*
>
> — THE DALAI LAMA

That opportunity is embodied in the Buddha's Third Noble Truth: "The cessation of suffering, through which it is explained that the causes of karma and the defilements can be removed."

Yes: The causes of karma can be removed.

Whew! That's better!

Okay, let's go over it again.

Actions produce karma. Negative actions produce negative karma. Positive actions produce positive karma. So it follows that eliminating the negative actions will eliminate the negative karma.

It sounds so simple! You're thinking: "All I have to do is stop being unkind or selfish and my suffering will end?"

It is that simple—but not that easy.

There are three kinds of actions, and each one is either virtuous or un-virtuous. The three categories of action are mental, verbal, and physical.

So karma is caused, not just by good or bad actions, but by good or bad thoughts and words as well. Which is good news and bad news! Considering how automatic our thoughts can be, how often and how quickly we jump to speak, how habitual our negative feelings can be, the suggestion simply to stop being un-virtuous is a tall order.

But that is the challenge and purpose of karma to begin with—overcoming the difficulties we encounter in order to learn and grow. Richard McLean claims that karma "urges us to act, to overcome old habits, and to accept responsibility for ourselves today, despite the past" (*Zen Fables for Today*, 1998). Joel Whitton agrees: "In the between-life state the soul reviews its performance across many lifetimes and chooses to resolve or atone for certain deeds in the next life" (*Life Between Life*, 1986).

As we know, "the past" goes much further back in time than just this lifetime. The past stretches backward into seemingly endless dimensions of past life. The knowledge that karma follows us, not just through this lifetime, but also through many others can be daunting.

So karma is like an eternal card game. Life after life, we hold these cards and plan our moves. Sometimes we make good decisions and win the hand; sometimes we make bad decisions and win the hand in that life—but not in a karmic sense.

However we choose, we carry these decisions from lifetime to lifetime, recreating the same situations over and over until we learn from them and release the energy and the karma around that energy. Karma isn't a punishment; it is a lesson to learn as quickly or as slowly as we choose.

Again, we choose how we handle the karmic hand we're dealt. We can learn "as quickly or as slowly as we wish."

You may be thinking: "How am I supposed to choose to learn my lessons if I can't remember what I did wrong in the first place?!"

This is where past-life regression comes in. Whether the journeys are real or a metaphor that the mind makes up—it doesn't matter. Whether we live in the past, present, or future, or whether time is all now, at one time . . . again, it doesn't matter. What does matter is which part of ourselves we use in each lifetime. Are we kind? Are we harsh and thoughtless? Do we live a life of empty self-absorption? Or do we take care of those around us? In each life, there is a lesson to learn, and how we handle that lesson becomes our karma . . . becomes what we take into our next—or current—lifetime. As Anthony de Mello warns: "My experience is that it's precisely the ones who don't know what to do with this life who are all hot and bothered about what they are going to do with another life ("Awareness: The Perils and Opportunities of Reality," in Stroud [ed], *The Illusion of Rewards*, 1992).

The Four Powers

Perhaps the best news in all of this is that, once you remember the past actions that may have created your karma, it is possible to clear and correct that karma. But even if you never have a past-life regression and you never remember anything about your previous incarnations, it is still possible to resolve negative karma from the past and create positive karma for the future.

Buddhism calls the keys to clearing karma The Four Powers of Purification: the power of the object, the power of regret, the power of promise, and the power of practice. Consider the parallels to twelve-step programs, which pledge the participant to be mindful, remorseful, and to seek redemption for past mistakes.

1. **Power of the Object:** Think of all beings you may have hurt (Step 4—Make a searching and fearless moral inventory of yourself). You don't have to know all the specifics; if you can't remember, just imagine. Chances are that, whatever wrongs you have had done to yourself in this life are the wrongs that you did to others in a past life. Karma is nothing if not perfectly just.

2. **Power of Regret:** Feel sorrow for the negative actions you have done (Step 1—Admit you are powerless over your addiction—that your life has become unmanageable, and Step 5—Admit to God, to yourself, and to another human being the exact nature of your wrongs). This does not mean that you should wrack yourself

with guilt. Guilt is always a waste of time and energy! You simply examine your actions and recognize that the negative ones were unwise.

3. **Power of Promise:** This is where you promise not to repeat the negative actions. Sincerity is very important here. You can't really say you'll *never* do something again. We all make mistakes. But you have to put genuine effort into not repeatedly making the same mistakes (Step 8 — Make a list of all persons you have harmed, and become willing to make amends to them all).

4. **Power of Practice:** Basically, doing good deeds is "good practice" (Step 9 — Make direct amends to such people wherever possible, except when to do so would injure them or others, and Step 10 — Continue to take personal inventory and when you are wrong promptly admit it).

So it's good news! We're not locked into our negative karma. We have the ultimate power to create good karma. It may not be easy. But the important thing is that it is possible.

So let's not continue thinking that karma is some sort of dominatrix who follows us around for all eternity to make sure that we suffer! Karma is more like a tough-love mom, holding us to the consequences of our actions and choices until we see the right way to behave. Karma wants us to learn and grow so that we can feel a gentle kindness and understanding toward all living things, including ourselves! That kind of boundless, all-encompassing love is the human soul in its purest, most powerful, and most peaceful state.

This is why karma clings to us until we learn. All we have to do is see it, understand it, and act in the interests of preserving the best of it. If we do that, all of our lives are transformed.

Consider This:

- Where has karma influenced your life?

- What hand of cards did you come in with?

- How well do you believe you've played those cards?

- What can you do differently/better in the future?

Chapter 5

What Is This State We Call Death?

Death is not extinguishing the light; it is only putting out the lamp because the dawn has come.

— RABINDRANATH TAGORE

In our culture, we have learned to fear death as the cessation of life—the end of pleasure, of experience, of all that we know on this earth. Science has taught us to believe that human death is a terminal state, a state of oblivion, a void that swallows life up forever, depriving us of redemption or the chance to make amends.

When you "flat line" on the EEG, your heart stops beating and all brain activity ceases. This is the scientific definition of death.

Because it represents the end of everything, death is often seen, by those who suffer unbearable pain or anguish, as a release or an escape from their suffering. For them, death is a welcome sleep, a state of unconsciousness, the lack of a felt reality.

For others, however, death is not an end, nor is life just a beating heart and measurable brainwave activity. It is a training ground in which we learn the art of dying so that we can live again. For these people, life never dies. Ormond McGill (*Grieve No More, Beloved*, 2003) gives this sage advice:

> Appreciate that basically life is a preparation for dying, and truly only those are wise who learn during life how to die, for in this "knowing" you come to understand the deepest meaning of life.

We know from the experience of those who provide palliative care that death is not simply an end to life. Following are some direct quotes from care providers who were present at the time of a death:

"I just felt him slip away . . . suddenly the room was empty, even though the body was there."

"Sometimes you can actually see the soul leave the body. You can certainly sense it. It's like a whisper of sound or movement, and then a stillness."

"When her daughter arrived from Vancouver, her dying mother said: 'I've been waiting for you.' They spoke for a while, and then her mother quietly closed her eyes, and stopped breathing."

"When they fight it out of fear, the death process can be very difficult for the patient; but for most, they welcome it with a smile or sense of its being the right time. And they just leave."

"Many of my patients say they see light, or someone they love standing at the foot of the bed, smiling, kind, and full of light, waiting to take them home."

Robert Thurman, in his translation of the *Tibetan Book of the Dead*, states that our scientific definition of death is neither accurate nor complete.

The illusion of the subjective "I" in the individual consciousness, assumed by materialists to correspond with the presence of brain wave activity, should cease with the cessation of brain waves. Yet the picture of death as nothing in consciousness is not a scientific finding. It is a conceptual notion. There are many cases of people being revived after "flatlining" for some time, and they report intense subjective experiences.

Thurman goes on to say that "a considerable body of credible evidence supports the probability of post-death existence of consciousness and sentient future life continuity." In other words, there is life after death.

I remember that, when my aunt died, she chose to leave in the middle of the afternoon—sitting and watching television. I was at my clinic and unreachable for a few hours.

> *He not busy being born is busy dying.*
>
> —Bob Dylan, "It's Alright Ma, I'm Only Bleeding"

That night, I saw her very clearly, and she said: "Remember I love you, and remember I'll always guide you in what colors you need to wear to look your best." She was an artist and very sure of her sense of fashion and color—and not so sure of mine! Three years later, she came to me one morning as I woke from sleep and said: "You're safe now, and your health is better, so I can move on." She smiled and disappeared. I felt blessed, but sadly alone. She still comes from time to time; I see her and feel pure love emanating from her smile. I feel blessed.

Near-Death Experiences

There have been many recorded statements of "near-death experiences" from people who were declared clinically dead and were revived. Many report the experience of being in a tunnel and moving toward a bright light. They are aware that they are about to cross over into another realm, and that this other realm represents death. They report feeling joy and relief, followed by disappointment when they are "yanked" back into life.

According to Dolores Cannon in *Between Death and Life* (1995), "What they're describing is what they see up to the approach to the barrier between the physical and the spiritual . . . this bright light is the barrier itself . . . "

What they are experiencing is the shift of vibration in the energy field as it starts to leave the denseness of the body.

When We Die

There is no cure for birth and death save to enjoy the interval.

— George Santayana

In order to understand what happens to us after we die, we need to understand the nature of energy and how it behaves.

According to the first law of thermodynamics, energy can neither be created nor destroyed. Nothing is new in the universe. What we constantly see are different formations of the same atoms.

So it is with the cosmos. We are not separate from the world. In *The Beginner's Guide for the Recently Deceased* (2004), David Staume argues:

> Although we perceive separate "things," they're like rain, steam, snow, rivers, and clouds—all water, all somewhere in the cycle of either issuing from or returning to the sea, and separate from it only in appearance . . .
>
> Our wonderful cosmos is such a system, an indivisible system. Fortunately, no matter how poor our descriptions or weak our analogies, the two principles that arise from this are clear: first, nothing is in any sense truly separate from anything else; and second, the whole is enfolded in every part.

Many things that were separate in the physical world merge in the astral world quite naturally. Sight, hearing, taste, and smell, for example, emanate from the same place. So to hear is to see, to smell is to hear, and to see is to smell. Just as things previously seen as separate and distinct in the physical world have been revealed by physics to be facets of the same thing—matter and energy, space and time, waves and particles—so in the astral world, every part contains within it the wisdom of the cosmos.

Our physical bodies are connected to our astral bodies by a silver cord that is a type of energy. When we die and we go through the "bright light," that cord is severed because we are passing through an intense energy field. When we go through this energy barrier, we are aware of a bright energy that cleanses us and adjusts our spiritual vibrations to be compatible with the spiritual level we have attained.

Experiments indicate that the mind, or consciousness, is not a physical object like the brain. The brain receives information that the consciousness gathers and then proceeds to translate it into thoughts and ideas. But it's the consciousness that identifies, categorizes, and generally organizes the information received. It is also believed that this information-processing function is independent of the constraints of time and space. "Many psychologists and neurologists," claims Migene González-Wippler, "suspect that the electromagnetic field that is the mind, and can be identified as human thought processes, may well function independently of the brain" (*What Happens After Death*, 1997).

Once we are on the other side, we may see scenes that resemble things we remember on the physical plane, but they seem much more beautiful to us. Gradually, we begin to realize that these are constructs of our own minds and we are seeing only what our minds are ready for. Eventually, we are ready to see things as they truly are.

> We do not die because we have to die; we die because one day, and not so long ago, our consciousness was forced to deem it necessary.
>
> —ANTONIN ARTAUD

Consider This:

- How do you feel about dying?

- What runs through your emotional and intellectual circuits when you consider what death may feel like?

Chapter 6

You and Your Past Lives

You've inherited most from yourself, not from your family.

—EDGAR CAYCE

Have you ever met anyone about whom you seem to know a lot, even though you've never met that person before? A new brother-in-law? Your child's teacher? I met my husband's cousin more than thirty years ago. Newly married, I discovered by chance that she was in the same city and in the hospital with a new baby. My husband had never mentioned this cousin; in fact, he barely spoke of his family at all. But for some reason, I felt that meeting her would be important. It has been. The husband? Long gone. The cousin? A close, warm, loving part of my life forever. We knew each other immediately, she and I, and so it has remained through the ups and downs of life—children growing, good and bad health, sadness, and celebrations. Thank you, karma! And, yes, she is part of my soul circle.

◆

Are you drawn to visit or live in a place you've never seen? Spain? Kenya? Are there other periods of history with which you feel you're aligned—the Crusades or the French Revolution—even though you have no apparent connection to them? Many times, clients come into the clinic and tell us they have just come back from Edinburgh or Brazil, Amsterdam or Kenya, and had the strangest sensation of knowing they were home. The place felt familiar and, in many cases, they could find their way around the old cities without a guide—they just "knew" where to go. One client visiting Hastings—a seaside resort in Britain—told of having an overwhelming sense of fear when they moved into their 16th-century hotel. When we subsequently went through a past-life regression journey, she found that she had been a foot soldier on the battlefield during the Battle of Hastings in 1066 and had died a cruel, painful death. The hotel was later built on the original battlefield.

◆

Have you had an affinity for a language that none of your family speaks or that is not part of your known heritage? I know someone who was born and raised in Sault Ste Marie, a small town in Eastern Canada, who always had a desire to learn Japanese. He came to Toronto not knowing any Japanese people, but found someone with whom he could exchange language skills. He picked Japanese up very quickly and now speaks it fluently. He is a blond-haired, blue-eyed, Japanese-speaking Canadian who, when we did the regression, became a Japanese housewife in two separate centuries. The first time he entered the Japanese past life, he started to weep because his/her feet were hurting so badly. They had been bound, as was the custom then. As a young teenage girl, her bones wanted to grow, but the bindings restricted growth and blood flow to the point of agony. The second Japanese life was more recent, but she was of the servant class, so there was no issue around the binding of feet.

◆

Have you always been fascinated by certain objects or music—Indian art or the violin—even though it hasn't got anything to do with your upbringing or family heritage? We see this, or hear about it, more and more with the proliferation of YouTube and TV talent shows. Young children have singing voices way beyond their years, sounding as if they've been trained by operatic singing teachers, when in fact, most of them just "heard it" and copied it. Most often, no one in the family has that talent. It comes from somewhere—and in most cases, that "somewhere" isn't DNA!

◆

Is there a place, or are there places, in the world that you absolutely dislike, even though you've never been there? Or repeatedly choose not to go

I did not begin when I was born nor when I was conceived. I have been growing, developing, through incalculable myriads of millenniums. . . . All my previous selves have their voices, echoes, promptings in me. . . . Oh, incalculable times again shall I be born.

—Jack London, The Star Rover

there? The basement of your house, or a hospital, or a doctor's office? This also applies to elevators, balconies of high-rise buildings, and tunnels for viewing stalactites. If you have an irrational fear and it doesn't run in your family, there is a strong likelihood that it comes from a past-life experience.

◆

Have you always wanted to climb Mount Everest, even though you grew up on the plains of Saskatchewan or Minnesota? Why do some people have such a strong connection to the sea, or to the mountains? They feel drawn to live in an environment that has nothing to do with their family origins or lifestyle. "I only feel at peace in the mountains." "Lakes don't do it for me—it has to be salt water." "I need the hustle and bustle of city noise; the peace and quiet in the country drives me crazy." These are direct comments from clients who hadn't thought about where these proclivities came from—they just knew that, for them, it was fact.

◆

Is there an unusual scar or birthmark on your body that's un-explainable? That perhaps even appeared during the first year after your birth? One spine-tingling version of this happened during a past-life regression training course. My students had just returned from a practice session and were recounting their experiences. There were fifteen people in the class; two experienced a time on a battlefield, on horseback, wearing armor. They were both killed by being knocked off their horses by a lance strike to the shoulder and a death stab through the back as they fell. Both claimed to have birthmarks on their backs below the shoulder. They realized that they both had been in the same battle and had been killed at the same time — by each other's foot soldiers. Chills! Silence in the room. And then tears. They hadn't known each other before this class — but from that moment, a deep and lasting friendship began.

◆

Have you had persistent phantom pain for as long as you can remember in any part of your body? A nagging ache around one eye, or a sharp pain in a shoulder, or a constant pain that comes and goes in exactly the same spot for no apparent reason? As I mentioned in the Introduction to this book, my horrific migraines were released through past-life regression healing, understanding, and forgiveness. There have been many other examples of this, most often when there's a part of the client's body that is particularly vulnerable — a shoulder, an elbow, an ankle. It always seems to be that part of the body that gets damaged or injured.

◆

Have you had any fears since early childhood that have no explainable source? Green-backed turtles (and you've never, ever, seen one, let alone been in the country they inhabit), or budgie birds, or goldfish? A few years ago, we did a research project in the clinic involving allergies to animals, or irrational fear of animals. And we found that just under 80 percent of these came from a past-life experience. Frightened of cats? Maybe you were hunted down as a witch in a previous life and, when caught, were tied into a sack with cats and drowned. Imagine the panic and pain that could cause! No wonder it gave you a phobia! The same is true of a fear of snakes or birds . . . something, somewhere in your psyche cries out in alarm from an old memory.

♦

Do you have a recurring dream that's so vivid that you feel that you're partly there all the time? Some people see choices in their lives, visualizing themselves turning left and seeing what happens differently, or having a conversation before it actually happens an hour or two later . . . and then the story is completed in dreamland. This could be what we call "lucid dreaming," or it could be that you're slipping between times—the then and the now.

Then you've quite possibly experienced these phenomena in another lifetime.

So as through a glass and darkly
The age long strife I see
Where I fought in many guises,
Many names—but always me.
—General George S. Patton

Why Do We Choose the Lives We Choose?

It's conceivable that I might be reborn as a Chinese coolie.
In such a case I should lodge a protest.
—Sir Winston Churchill

We choose the lives we live because of the lesson(s) we need to learn. Sometimes people have difficulty regressing into a past life because they have an issue or issues that need to be dealt with in this lifetime before they can move back and explore other lifetimes. But in general, of the people in my experience who request past-life regression—many of whom have never been hypnotized before—over 90 percent have traveled without difficulty into a past-life regression.

> To everything there is a season, and a time to every purpose under the heaven: a time to be born and a time to die; a time to plant, and a time to pluck up that which is planted; a time to kill, and a time to heal; a time to break down, and a time to build up; a time to weep, and a time to laugh; a time to mourn and a time to dance; a time to cast away stones, and a time to gather stones together; a time to embrace, and a time to refrain from embracing; a time to get, and a time to lose; a time to keep, and a time to cast away; a time to rend, and a time to sew; a time to keep silence, and a time to speak; a time to love, and a time to hate; a time of war, and a time of peace.
>
> —Ecclesiastes 3:1–8

Occasionally, when people are curious about a particular interest they have—say, for instance, ancient Chinese block prints—and they decide they want to explore it further, their souls may decide that it is not the appropriate place for them to go first. It may take them somewhere else to learn the appropriate lessons before taking them to ancient China.

In the earliest recorded instance of the near-death phenomenon, 731 AD, the historian Bede (c. 672–735) wrote, in his *History of the English Church and People*:

A man from the province of Northumbria returns from the dead . . . "A handsome man in a shining robe was my guide . . . He said to me . . . 'You must now return to your body and live among men once more; but, if you will weigh your actions with greater care and study to keep your words and ways virtuous and simple, then when you die you too will win a home among these happy spirits that you see' . . . I was most reluctant to return to my body . . . but I did not dare to question my guide. Meanwhile, I know not how, I suddenly found myself alive among men once more." . . . [I]nspired by an insatiable longing for the blessings of heaven, and by his words and by his life, he helped many people to salvation.

Past-Life Regression — What It Is *Not*

Reincarnation is making a comeback.
— SEEN ON A LAPEL BADGE IN BRITAIN

Past-life regression is not a party game, nor is it something that's done by one person to another. It's not necessary to be psychic or "special" or "weird" to experience past lives.

Past-life regression is not somebody else's version of your experience. People occasionally come into the clinic and tell me: "I was told by someone that I lived another life as a healer (or a high priest)." This has nothing to do with past-life regression. It's somebody else's interpretation of your energy.

Many clairvoyants can see past lives as they work with a client, but it is important to remember that the interpretation is theirs and not yours! An ethical clairvoyant will suggest that you find a past-life regression therapist so that you can experience the journey and gain the wisdom and healing it brings.

I came into one of my past lives as a young boy of maybe nine or ten, playing an ancient big-bellied guitar-type instrument. I was dressed in the manner we might expect of a court jester—soft pointed shoes, colored hose and short pants, a diamond-shaped leather jerkin over a white shirt with large, billowing sleeves. A stocking cap was on my head with a tassel at the end. But my job was to play music and sing to a group of ladies having tea. These ladies wore huge, colorful skirts and had high white wigs on their heads. There were jewels around their necks and on their wigs. The room was large, with tables dotted here and there, and servants passing out the tea and cake. I had to circulate and sing my songs.

After doing this for a few months, I realized that no one was listening to my music or my songs. But if I stopped, I was called into the kitchen and beaten by the head footman, and then sent back to sing until the ladies left. Later on, I learned how to amuse myself. Once I realized that no one was listening to me, I made up songs about the ladies—what they were wearing, their voices, the gossip that passed from table to table, those who ate too much who shouldn't, and those who were spindle thin and ate nothing.

Eventually, when I was no longer pleasing to the eye (I became older and stooped), they transferred me to the children's courtyard, where I was once again told to play my music. And again, no one cared about or listened to my music, so it was a lonely time. But I did enjoy watching the children laugh and play.

The wisdom from that life was, for me, profound. The music is still the music, even if no one listens.

The vast majority of people experience past lives that may seem mundane or boring to the listener, but that, for the individual, may bring the answer they are seeking. I've never yet had clients who, in a past life, had actually been Cleopatra, Queen Elizabeth I, or Leonardo da Vinci; but I have had people who lived during those lifetimes and could record what they saw and felt about that person—from a slave's, or a soldier's, or peddler's point of view. "It is human to be intrigued and flattered by the possibility that you were once powerful, rich, talented or famous," J. H. Brennan warns in *The Reincarnation Workbook* (1989). "It may even be that it is exactly the sort of news you most desperately need to hear in order to compensate for your perceived shortcomings in this life." We must remember, however, that each person's story is unique and special, whatever their role or name in that lifetime.

I once worked with a client who was convinced she had been Cleopatra and wanted past-life regression to prove it. Because of the prior assumption on her part, I was even more vigilant than usual in questioning and recording the journey. During the session, I began asking questions she couldn't answer. She replied: "I'm not getting that information." She also missed out on some very important but little-known data and could only come up with the highlights of Cleopatra's love life with Mark Antony. Her body language was incongruent during the session, and so was the energy

I received from her. Her language and voice were much too theatrical and aggressive.

In normal trance, the client is almost motionless, with REM (Rapid Eye Movement) apparent under the eyelids; the voice is usually low and, even when imperious, more muted than usual. This client was physically animated—the whole experience was like a movie script being played out.

After the "Cleopatra" lifetime, while she was still relaxed, I deepened the hypnosis and took her into another lifetime in which she was a pioneer wife and mother traveling across the West in a wagon train. Her whole demeanor changed. Eye movement, breath, voice, and diction lowered and slowed down. She gave off a relaxed and clean energy. When she came back to the surface, she was pleased about the Cleopatra event, but clearly and visibly moved by the pioneer story. I told her that I believed that, sometimes, a part of us wishes to have the attributes of a famous person so much that we align ourselves subconsciously with that person. In NLP (neuro-linguistic programming), we call that modeling. But in past-life journeys, we understand it is a copy, not the real thing.

Reincarnation is not an exclusively Hindu or Buddhist concept, but it is part of the history of human origin. It is proof of the mindstream's capacity to retain knowledge of physical and mental activities.

It is related to the theory of interdependent origination and to the law of cause and effect.

—THE DALAI LAMA, THE CASE FOR REINCARNATION

Reincarnation is not an idea dreamed up by those who wish to escape their fear of dying. It's not a quick way back to the land of the living, or an answer to our wish for immortality.

It's not important whether a past-life experience takes place in another time or another place, or whether it's a metaphor designed by your subconscious mind to allow you to experience healing or wisdom. What is important is that past-life regression gives us the opportunity for a new and clean start—another chance to learn and grow toward our goal of spiritual betterment.

Healing Ourselves

My hope is that you keep your mind open. It is not hyp-notherapists who heal, it is you who have the ultimate responsibility. Hypnosis allows you to expand and explore your awareness and eliminate fear, anxiety, depression, and other negative tendencies, as well as the fear of death.
— BRUCE GOLDBERG

Past-life memories come to us in many guises: déjà vu; recurrent dreams (either of a specific location or a frightening event); a crippling phobia, or unexplained, groundless fear. People who fear water, public speaking, or heights (to name just a few common phobias) often uncover the memory of a death by drowning, hanging, or burning at the stake, or falling from a high place. As these past-life traumas are explored and resolved in therapy, the phobias cease to exist.

Emotional and physical challenges carried over from past incarnations into the present life can be quickly and effectively resolved through past-life regression therapy in far fewer sessions than with conventional therapy. Many physical ailments are considered to be psychosomatic, and these conditions may diminish or cease altogether through past-life regression therapy. Winafred Blake Lucas, in her book, *Regression Therapy Book II* (1996), adds:

> If we were locked into the patterns of emotion and thought that are set in place during our gestation, we would be prisoners of our history, controlled by a forgotten past. However, bringing our prebirth memories to consciousness through regression leads to a liberation from early negative experiences and to increased autonomy and freedom of choice. We can jettison our subconscious scripts. When the therapy is concluded, emotional limitations are lifted and the potential for personal fulfillment is increased.

In the prologue to her book *Past Lives, Future Healing* (2000), Sylvia Browne tells of a man who underwent therapy of various kinds, including medication, for four years to deal with extreme panic and agoraphobia. Past-life regression revealed that he had been poisoned in a past life and that his agoraphobia was triggered by an episode in a grocery store in which the word "poison" was used.

Psychiatrist Dr. Brian L. Weiss, author of *Many Lives, Many Masters* (1988), tells a similar story of a patient of his who struggled for more than a year in conventional psychotherapy to get to the root of her many fears and phobias. Still severely impaired, she consented to try hypnosis in an attempt to discover if childhood traumas could be causing her problems. During one of these sessions, she regressed into a past life, much to the surprise of Dr. Weiss, and, after recalling events in other past lives, her symptoms began to improve dramatically. These sessions not only helped his patient, but also changed Dr. Weiss's life. He went on to do ground-breaking research in past-life therapy. "As a therapist or a patient," he wrote in *Through Time Into Healing* (1993), "you don't have to believe in past lives or reincarnation for past life therapy to work. The proof is in the pudding. As more than one fellow psychotherapist has said to me, 'I still don't know if I believe in this past life stuff, but I use it, and it sure does work!'"

Some Questions You May Ask Yourself

I wonder what I was begun for, seeing as I am so soon done for.

—INSCRIPTION ON A GRAVESTONE OF A LITTLE GIRL,
WREXHAM, WALES

The following are questions that are commonly raised by my clients and by others considering past-life regression.

Can We Become Other Life Forms?

Yes. We can live life in many forms—as an animal or even as an element like wind or rain. It is generally thought that animals have a universal soul or consciousness, but from time to time, I have experienced people taking on an animal shape or incarnation if they need to learn the lesson of that life. For instance, one of my clients became a snake and went through the skin-shedding process to learn that it was time for him to move into a new iteration in his life. Another client briefly took the form of an eagle to learn that she had to move away from the minutiae of a relationship and into a wider view of the beauty and power of the world of the relationship. Many people who go on shamanic journeys take the form of an animal so that they may experience the wisdom that an animal can impart. I personally see this process as just another form of that.

Can We Come from or Go to Another Planet?

Yes, we can, and we do! Some of our clients and students have experienced lives on Atlantis and Lemuria. One in particular was on a red planet where he was a scientist who worked to prevent the planet from imploding. But he learned that what he was trying to do was too little too late.

Can We Live Simultaneous Lifetimes?

There are different points of view on this. I personally believe that we cannot. I believe that we each have one soul that, from time to time, may be fragmented through trauma. But it is just one soul living one life at a time. Each soul comes to this planet to experience the various lives it needs to in order to progress.

How Many Past Lives Have I Had?

There's no way of knowing. Just as there's no way of knowing how many you have yet to live. Every time you live a life, you live it to learn the experience and the wisdom it brings. And if you don't learn the lesson, guess what? You do it again, to learn the same lesson, over and over, until you get it.

Consider This

- Where have you been, or whom have you met that seemed familiar to you—even though the meeting was a new experience?

- How do you feel about the idea of having lived before?

- When you dream, do you see yourself differently? How?

Chapter 7

Your Soul and Soul Mates

A soul mate is someone who has locks that fit our keys,
and keys to fit our locks.

— Richard Bach

There are two overarching questions around relationships that people always want answered. The questions go something like this: "Is there a perfect mate out there for me?" or "Will I meet my soul mate?"

When most people think of soul mates, they think in terms of "forever," "life partner," and "two halves of one whole." People think a soul mate is their one and only true love. But in reality, this type of connection is shared between "twin flames," not soul mates. I'll talk about twin flames a little later on— although they're not really part of the soul circle.

As human beings, we instinctively yearn for this kind of intimate connection with another. For most people, if they're not happily partnered, then they're looking to be happily partnered. We're always on the lookout for that one person who will "complete" us.

However, meeting your "soul mate" is not always synonymous with meeting your life partner or lover.

Soul-mate relationships are not necessarily romantic relationships, and there is almost always more than one. Soul-mate relationships are common and plentiful. You could come across ten or twenty (or more) soul mates in your lifetime! These soul mates are considered by many to be part of your "soul circle" or "soul group." And your soul circle travels together with you through many lifetimes.

Soul Circles and Soul Mates

The soul circle plays an integral role in the Interlife and in the overall journey of each individual soul. On her website, *www.rachelkeene.co.uk*, Rachel Keene tells us that every person "has a group of souls we are spiritually connected to . . . a group we are meant to connect with in both the spirit world, and here by choice in physical form."

Remember from our discussion of the Interlife journey that your whole purpose for incarnating on earth is for spiritual growth. This is also the reason you are tied to a soul circle. Members of a soul circle enact soul contracts and agree to meet again on earth. They "come into our lives at seemingly random times," Keene argues, "but in fact these meetings were prearranged between us in spirit before we came here. We agree to connect and enable each other to learn a lesson or many lessons."

Very often, the first or second stop on the Interlife journey is the meeting with the soul circle. This is where you reconnect with your soul mates. There is an overwhelming feeling of joy and peace when you meet again after your physical death. These souls sometimes remain with you during the Interlife journey, welcoming you when you arrive, guiding you through the journey, and supporting you through your life review.

In 99 percent of the experiences clients have while journeying through the Interlife, their meetings with the soul group are often the most exciting for them. It is in this group of souls that they may meet people in their current lives or previous

> *He drifted off into sleep and Janie looked down on him and felt a self-crushing love. So her soul crawled out from its hiding place.*
>
> —Zora Neale Hurston, Their Eyes Were Watching God

lifetimes who have had a decided impact on the way they currently think or behave. There's often an instant recognition. Even though these souls may look like gatherings of light spots or shifting shapes, the recognition of their essence is profound. "My sister's here!" "My ex-husband—now that's weird." "There's Miss Harris, my third-grade teacher." And there may be others from previous lifetimes that clients may not recognize.

Clients learn, in the session, the role each soul plays in the soul circle—perhaps, for example, to bring balance. One may teach someone not to take her/himself so seriously.

Another may help in the understanding of cause and effect on behavior. Always, the circle is balanced with souls that bring what the client's soul needs along the journey. The soul circle can, and does, change as the needs change. So it's perfectly acceptable for an ex—or a narcissistic parent, or an overly demanding boss, or a nurturing friend, or a lover, or a grandparent—to be a soul mate. All have a role to play as providers of opportunity for the soul to grow, for the lesson to be learned. These are the true soul mates.

It's probably no surprise to learn that my mother is a member of my soul circle. And now I understand so much more. There is no way I could have grown or learned as I have without having experienced the emotional and physical pain of her parenting. And I now also understand that this was the role she took on in this lifetime, so that I could learn these lessons.

There are no accidents . . . there is only some purpose that we haven't yet understood.

—Deepak Chopra

The major purpose of soul groups is to help each individual soul learn and grow. That's why we're here. That's why we contract to meet each other again. Sometimes these relationships are happy; sometimes they are less than happy. Either way, soul-mate relationships are meant to teach us.

Often, people think a soul-mate relationship is, by definition, a romantic love relationship. Sometimes this is true; sometimes it's not. Soul mates can incarnate as friends, family, or total strangers.

What Is a Soul Mate?

Many clients who come to me are interested in finding their soul mates because, in their minds—thanks to books, magazines, television, and movies—they see a soul-mate relationship as two people immersed in the bliss of a deep love experience and that's what they believe. Even those already in a relationship wonder if their partners are soul mates, assuming it is the most profound heart connection they can find. Sometimes it is. Sometimes it isn't.

But, contrary to popular belief, soul-mate relationships are not the simple, glorious nirvana they are depicted to be. These relationships have captured our attention because they are filled with passion and growth, and therefore seem romantic. However, soul-mate relationships can be quite painful, despite—or because of—the frenzy of passion. As Rachel Keene tells us: "Quite often you will feel a pull towards that person which surpasses any emotional connection you could possibly have built up in the short time you have known them."

Understand: soul mates are ideal partners because they are souls who contracted to spend time together during their current incarnation. However, soul mates are also the most challenging relationships because they are purposely established to stimulate growth.

Soul-mate contracts are carefully discussed and initiated between future mates prior to their physical experience, during the Interlife, just as parental contracts are determined as you select the genetic pool and family environment that best support and maximize learning during your incarnate experience. This means that soul-mate contracts are often designed to assist you in experiencing lessons that are difficult.

You pick relationships with souls that can best stimulate your growth based on a strong karmic connection. In fact, it is likely that you will have issues left to resolve from prior lifetimes together. Or you and your soul mate may be well suited for resolving a key emotional issue you have resisted learning in the past. A soul mate is perfectly designed to push your buttons so he or she can boost you into new realms of realization. "What angers us in another person," Simon Peter Fuller explains, "is more often than not an unhealed aspect of ourselves. If we had already resolved that particular issue, we would not be irritated by its reflection back to us."

Soul-mate relationships are recognized by the passion they engender — otherwise, most human beings would never have the fortitude to connect or remain with these mates, since the interaction is often fraught with fiery conflict or spurts of sexual passion. This passion is often the glue that holds the union together as the two people work through the resolution of negative karma. It is the insurance that holds soul mates together during a roller-coaster ride through the heights of passion and the plunge to despair until the karmic work is completed.

When soul mates first meet, they sometimes feel as if they already know each other. They may feel very familiar to each other. Some soul-mate relationships may last a lifetime; others may only be for a particular purpose and may be temporary.

Regardless, all relationships serve a purpose and should be honored and appreciated for what they have to offer you in your personal spiritual growth. If you find yourself involved in one or more relationships that are causing ongoing chaos or pain, step back emotionally for a moment to consider the learning and the pattern(s) you may need to break. Thank the person and the experiences for all that you have had the opportunity to learn and to make a commitment to clear. Know that all relationships are sacred, because they bring us closer to the Light of All That Is.

So Who Is Your Soul Mate?

A soul mate is any person who comes into your life for a period of time to help you learn a lesson that will advance your spiritual growth. Period. A soul mate can be your father, your sister, your friend, your boss, your dentist, or the guy you buy your paper from every morning who starts your day off with a smile of recognition.

Soul mates pre-arrange their encounters in the space between lives. One soul agrees to help another soul evolve in a certain way by learning a particular lesson. When both souls are incarnated, they meet

I have learned silence from the talkative, tolerance from the intolerant and kindness from the unkind. I should not be ungrateful to those teachers.

—KAHLIL GIBRAN

to carry out their agreement. You don't have to worry about finding your soul mate. You will naturally find each other. This phenomenon is called the soul-mate contract. Meeting a soul mate is not a random event—it is an officially prearranged part of the cycle.

Included in this cycle are sub-contracts, so to speak, that you create with your soul mates. These soul-mate contracts ensure that the two of you will meet in the next lifetime.

So, once you do meet a soul mate, how will you know them? The very nature of a soul-mate relationship ensures that you'll connect with the person at the right time. There's no way you'd brush by a soul mate on the subway and never meet again. The fact that you are contracted with that person is an iron-clad guarantee that you will meet and benefit each other in some way. But there is more than this cosmic explanation for why you are drawn to your soul mates. There is a physical reason for it—an in-body experience. It's called the limbic brain.

The Limbic Brain

The limbic system is a network of nerves and glands within the human brain that "is a major center for emotion formation and processing, for learning, and for memory" (*www. stanford.edu/group/hopes/basics/braintut/ab5.html*).

The limbic system acts as a memory bank. It stores memories and emotional connections that occur from pre-birth to age three. It's where each of our unique emotional blueprints is formed at the cellular level. The information processed there becomes the basis for our current life's emotional reality.

Children are the most absorbent sponges nature ever created. Babies and children are constantly observing the connections among the adults who surround them. Until a child reaches age three, the limbic system is busy cataloging and recording every event into this memory bank.

Infants instinctively know that their caregivers are meant to treat them with love, dignity, and deep caring. They know on some level that they are helpless, and they rely on their caregivers to meet all their needs, both physical and emotional. They assume, following this primitive logic, that whatever type of care they receive represents what love truly is. "Children will educate themselves under right conditions," Anne Sullivan says about Helen Keller in *The Story of My Life* (1903). "They require guidance and sympathy far more than instruction."

These early experiences become models. We intuitively seek out whatever model we've assimilated into our subconscious minds. If your parents were distant and undemonstrative, you quickly take "distant and undemonstrative" as your definition of love. If your parents argued a lot, you learn that arguing means love. It becomes your karmic duty to settle these issues by working through them in your own relationships.

Encoded into our very brains is a pattern of behavior that we constantly try to recreate. This is where our soul mates come in.

I Felt an Instant Connection!

Many times, I've had people tell me about someone they've met or perhaps seen across the proverbial crowded room. They tell me about the instant connection they felt with this person, or how it seemed as if they knew the person already. They are convinced these are the signs of a soul-mate relationship. My belief, however, is that this is rarely the case.

Instead, these instant connections are simply the intuitive recognition of a familiar pattern. It's the limbic brain at work.

When we meet someone and feel an instant connection, it's usually because they carry out the pattern that matches our definition of love. Even though the person may not have uttered a single word or exhibited a single indicative behavior, we know, at a DNA level, that they are a pattern match.

Soul mates are the people who come into our lives to help us resolve old patterns. Let's face it—most of us are not brought up with perfect and pristine models of love. Most of us have old wounds that are rooted in these early relationships. It is our spiritual goal to overcome such wounds. Our soul mates help us do it.

I am like a falling star who has finally found her place next to another in a lovely constellation, where we will sparkle in the heavens forever.

—Amy Tan

In his book *The Little Soul and the Sun* (1998), Neale Donald Walsch allows a little soul to learn forgiveness in its next reincarnation. When the little soul asks how he can learn forgiveness if there is no one to forgive, another soul steps forward and offers to be the teacher. The little soul is amazed that a being of light would do this for him.

> "Don't be so amazed," said the Friendly Soul, "you have done the same thing for me. Don't you remember? Oh, we have danced together, you and I, many

times. Through the eons and across all the ages have we danced. Across all time and in many places have we played together. You just don't remember.

"We have both been All Of It. We have been the Up and Down of it, the Left and the Right of it. We have been the Here and the There of it, the Now and the Then of it. We have been the male and the female, the good and the bad—we have been both the victim and the villain of it.

"Thus we have come together you and I, many times before; *each* bringing to the *other* the exact and perfect opportunity to Express and to Experience Who We Really Are."

Your soul contract ensures that you'll meet your soul mates, and your limbic brain helps you recognize them.

Remember, soul mates can be anyone, not just romantic partners. They can be friends, siblings, coworkers, a holiday romance, even a virtual stranger you only meet for one day. Anyone who comes into your life and pushes your emotional buttons in any significant way is likely a contracted soul mate you agreed to connect with—and somehow learn from—in this lifetime.

> *The people we are in relationship with are always a mirror, reflecting our own beliefs, and simultaneously we are mirrors, reflecting their beliefs. A relationship with another human being is one of the most powerful tools for growth that we have.*
>
> —SHAKTI GAWAIN

If your soul mate is your romantic partner, it can be truly wonderful. But even if your partner isn't a soul mate, you can still have a deep, soulful connection that helps both of you to grow. In fact, mutual growth is an ideal blueprint for any relationship—particularly a love partnership.

Pizza Or a Gourmet Meal?

Soul-mate relationships are preparatory for the main event . . . the "perfect partner." A soul-mate contract simply indicates that you ordered the relationship prior to arrival. It is like a pizza delivery. You ordered it ahead of time so you could eat it when it arrived. However, it is not a five-course gourmet meal—i.e., a perfect partnership—that you are meant to savor slowly.

Recognize the preparatory work you have done in order to align with a perfect partner in balance, harmony, mutual uplifting, and love. For this is your final incarnate goal. Ultimately, when you connect with your perfect partner, you are ready to connect in a relationship that has the capacity to move both you and your mate to Divine Union with each other and with the universe.

The Perfect Partnership

The learning experience derived from soul mates, if the work is done properly, is an excellent catalyst for moving toward a more evolved level of relationship. A perfect partnership has no karma attached to it. This means that there are no prior imbalances from previous lifetimes together to resolve. The partnership is a mature one, characterized by balance, because both players are supporting the growth of themselves and each other without any resolution of past conflicts.

We have been led to believe that finding a soul mate is critical because he or she is our one and only ideal mate for this lifetime. If it is appropriate to your lifetime's experience, you will remain in your relationship with your soul mate past the point of resolution of karmic issues, evolving the soul-mate contract into a partnership contract. But if the relationship is not supporting your life experience, you will be impelled to move on to new relationships.

Divorce is actually an institution designed for a soul's fast growth, not the anathema of the family structure it is often positioned to be. Divorce allows you to complete a soul-mate contract and evolve to the next relationship. The longer you hold on to an inappropriate old relationship—because you know it and are familiar with it and are afraid that nothing new will surface—the less likely you will be to evolve eventually into the most pleasant relationship of all—a partnership relationship.

Subsequent relationships are often characterized by less frenzied passion but deeper love,

Life has taught us that love does not consist in gazing at each other, but in looking outward together in the same direction.
—Antoine de Saint-Exupéry

because we grow and mature through the earlier experiences. Moreover, the subsequent relationships usually have fewer karmic ties. You are not resolving past lifetime conflicts or moving through a multitude of current lessons in a perfect partnership. You are simply partnering with a mate to experience the balance made possible through your prior relationship work.

This does not mean that later relationships lack romance, or that you have grown old and lost your capacity for passion. It simply means that the intensity of the passion experienced in earlier relationships will be less necessary as you move into unions based on mutual support through trust and loving friendship.

Twin Flames

Twin flames are very different from soul mates, and are very rare. Twin flames are two people in two separate bodies that share the same soul. Twin flames meet each other in their first incarnation so that they remember the soul frequency of the other being. They are then usually reunited during their last time on this planet. If twin flames meet before they are ready, they can be the total opposite and not at all compatible. When twin flames meet and are ready for each other, it is the most enjoyable experience possible on earth.

At this point, twin flames are almost identical. They truly complement each other, and it is a hardship for them to be apart. For an outside observer, it is sometimes hard to distinguish the two people. They have a very strong bond and often experience telepathic communication with each other. Their lives, even before meeting each other, have many parallels. Again, meeting your twin flame is very rare on this planet.

Rescinding Soul-Mate Contracts

Yes, it's possible! But why would you want to break apart a soul contract?

Maybe you have decided to enter a lifetime with no soul-mate contracts, since this type of relationship is not pertinent to your chosen lessons. You are literally a free agent who can choose the relationships that feel best. However, if you have experienced soul-mate relationships prior to meeting your life partner, it is imperative to break those contracts formally.

Think of people you know who have broken up with a mate, but seem unable to let go of the relationship. It impacts their emotional balance, and it flavors their lives well past the point of separation. Perhaps you know an adult child who just cannot leave "the nest" either physically or emotionally. Or sibling groups that seem unnaturally close—to the exclusion of all other relationships—so that even their life partners feel like outsiders. This is because the soul-mate contracts are still in place. They were not broken when the karmic work was completed.

Soul-mate contracts are established in the Akashic or soul records based on vows that have been taken at the soul level. The vows must be rescinded in order to feel a release, in order to move to the next experience—both emotionally and spiritually—be it another relationship or a time of solitude. In fact, if your vows are not rescinded, you may very well encounter the same individual in another lifetime based on the continued existence of the Akashic-record contract. This is why some of you have entered relationships that did not feel quite right, yet you felt compelled to experience them. You are probably replaying a soul-mate contract left over from a prior lifetime.

This is not to say that you cannot learn from these experiences, since every situation brings growth. However, this unfinished business can sidetrack you from intended nurturing relationships.

If you are or have been in a prior soul-mate arrangement and feel you are not emotionally and spiritually released from it, it is time to rescind your vows. It is also appropriate to rescind your vows if you are currently in a soul-mate relationship that is characterized by ongoing drama—perhaps family issues or friendships, the upheaval of passion followed by conflict, resolution of conflict, more passion, and more resolution—and you can't seem to stop the cycle.

The disavowal of your soul-mate contract does not mean that you will no longer be together. It simply removes the karmic pull from your interactions with the other person (or group of people), which smoothes the friction in the relationship.

> *The real voyage of discovery consists not in seeing new landscapes, but in having new eyes.*
>
> —MARCEL PROUST

If you wish to end a soul contract, I have provided instructions at the end of this chapter.

Finding Your Soul Circle

One of the most amazing things about the otherworldly realm is that it's accessible to us even while we are still alive on earth. It is not necessary to die a physical death in order to visit there, meet your soul group, and gain knowledge about your life's higher purpose. Hypnotherapy is one way to access this sacred place within yourself. I have provided a Soul Circle Meditation Script for self-recording at the end of chapter nine, so even if you don't have access to a regression facilitator, you can use self-hypnosis or meditation to tune in to the spiritual realm.

Soul-mate and soul-circle relationships are the most challenging and the most spiritually rewarding relationships you'll ever have. The friend who demeans you, the boyfriend who cheats, the mother who is somehow both overbearing and distant—these kinds of maddening relationships are usually the most significant ones, because they force you to look honestly at yourself, who you believe yourself to be, and what you really need and want in a relationship for your future.

Soul-mate relationships aren't always loving in nature, and often they don't last an entire lifetime. But this is not a detriment; soul mates are meant to help you learn a lesson. Once they've done what they came to do, they go. Once you understand this, you can be aware of it happening. You'll then be able to accept and appreciate whatever terms the soul-mate contract requires.

> *As human beings, our greatness lies not so much in being able to remake the world . . . as in being able to remake ourselves.*
>
> —MAHATMA GANDHI

Your primary soul circle is with you eternally, although its members can change from time to time. Some souls in your circle learn everything they need to learn and are able to "ascend" into a new circle with more advanced lessons. Some soul mates skip a lifetime and appear in your next. Whatever the circumstance, these are the most valuable relationships you will ever have. They literally make you who you are. Soul-circle relationships are sacred and powerful. As are you! You also are a member of the soul circles of others you encounter in your lifetime.

How to Rescind a Soul Contract

If ending a soul contract interests you, here's how to do it. First, you need to take yourself into a hypnotic trance or meditation to connect with your higher self.

1. Ask your guides if it is appropriate for you to rescind your soul-mate vows at this time. If you have not yet resolved all of the past karma between you and your partner, you will not be permitted to rescind the vow. You can also use a pendulum if it is easier for you to dowse for a yes or no answer.

2. Once you have agreement to go ahead, light a white candle and cup your hands, palms down, over the flame, (not too close!) asking the energy from the white light to clear your energy field and create a place of balance from where you can make your request. Ask your guides and teachers to join you and to assist you in rescinding your vows made with (name of soul mate you are letting go). Bear in mind that you can only release someone through love. Anger doesn't cut it as a release, since it

creates a magnet that bonds energy rather than dissolving it.

3. Imagine bringing the white light from the candle through to your body, and ask that Creator Love, Light, and Truth be present throughout your physical, spiritual, mental, and emotional being as you make your request.

4. Mentally envision the partner you are releasing and bring your hands over your heart, conjuring the intense and heightened feeling (of the love) you initially felt when you entered the relationship, prior to the conflict. Sometimes, envisioning this person as a child makes it easier to feel this love energy.

5. Hold the love energy in your hands and move your hands over your head, palms up. Release the energy into the atmosphere.

     Say: "I acknowledge the love I have felt for (name) in the past. I retain that feeling of love while releasing the emotional chord that continues to bind me to (name)." After stating these words, envision the severing of a silver cord that connects your heart to your previous partner's heart. Bring your end of the silver cord into your own heart by reeling it in, as you might do to retrieve a fishing line. Feel the release of your energy from that of your partner.

6. After extinguishing the candle flame, complete the ritual by saying: "So let it be."

7. You may need to do this a few times until you feel the release happening.

Consider This:

- Who in your life could be a soul mate? Who helped you to grow and learn? And what did you learn? Remember, it doesn't have to be positive!

- Whom do you think you are helping to learn and grow at a soul level?

Chapter 8

What Is the Interlife?

Behind Me—dips Eternity—
Before Me—Immortality—
Myself—the Term between—

—EMILY DICKINSON

In the many years during which I have regressed thousands of people, both into past lives and the Interlife, or the life between lives, I have always been challenged with the question: How do I know what I experienced is real?

At the risk of sounding like a Jesuit scholar or a Kabbalist, I will answer the question with another question: What do you mean by real?

Does your definition of "real" mean things you do every day? Or things and events you've heard about from somewhere or someone else?

What I have discovered is that, as you learn to experience and understand more and more about death and rebirth—the exploration of the Interlife—you connect more strongly and more profoundly with your current lifetime. Over time, I've noted that the people I say I care for, I really do care for— the others just drift away. The memories that are glorious stay around, while the not-so-glorious drift away (except when I recall them for my writings). The life itself becomes more precious, more intent-full, and more that of choice.

Why is that? Exploration allows growth and understanding—for the same reason that the more you travel to other countries, the more you interact with other cultures, the more you embrace your own. We bring the eagle-eye view to everything we encounter—whether we encounter it physically, emotionally, or spiritually.

And truly, the eagle-eye view is what you get when you journey through the Interlife or Life between Lives of your soul journey.

So What *Is* the Interlife?

If you believe in reincarnation in nature—the seed of a plant recycling through the seasons, for instance—then you also believe that it is so with us. The seed of who you are leaves one body and returns in another. And if you don't believe in reincarnation, then allow the journey to be considered as a metaphor created by your mind to bring healing and understanding. Are you okay with that?

Think of it as one door opening and another closing. "Understand this," notes Ormond McGill in *Grieve No More, Beloved* (2003), "death is a door. It is not a stopping. Awareness (consciousness) moves, but your body remains at the door. The body is left outside the temple, but your Awareness enters the temple." But what about the corridor between the doors? What about the time between these incarnated life-times?

We enter a place that the *Tibetan Book of the Dead* calls Bardo, or, as others call it, the Interlife, or the Labyrinth, or the Blue Mist of Life between Lives.

In *Life Between Life* (1986), Joel Whitton describes this as "metaconsciousness," a state of memory awareness in which we merge into existence itself, causing us to lose all sense of personal identity, while at the same time becoming more in-tensely self-aware than ever. He explains that

> while this might suggest an atmosphere of free-floating,
> cottonwool emptiness, the life between life is not a
> fairy-tale world. Those who have tasted its richness know
> that they have visited the ultimate reality, the plane
> of consciousness from which we embark on successive
> trials of incarnation and to which we return at the death
> of the body.

Within this space, this place, is a journey of discovery on which you may meet your soul circle, discover your immortal name, and learn your soul color. You may journey to a labora-tory or school for more learning. You may go to a place of rest or soul relaxation to heal and recover from a trau-matic incarnation. You will probably meet your coun-cil of advisors and go to a place to choose your next incarnation. You will find

Leaving this life is just like going from one room to another and closing the door.

—DAVID BRANDT BERG

out why you have to reincarnate—the purpose of your current life and why you chose the body you currently inhabit.

The first time I took an Interlife journey, I was informed that I chose the body I currently inhabit because it was strong and serviceable and would allow me to do the work I was meant to do. Not very glamorous, but realistic! (And I've always wanted to be taller, with long blond hair and long straight legs . . . Oh well, maybe next time.)

Does everyone take the same journey? No. But all journeys are remarkably similar, even if the journeyperson has never discussed the concept previously, or read anything about traveling to the Interlife. According to Winafred Blake Lucas in *Regression Therapy: A Handbook for Professionals* (1996), Interlife experiences are under our conscious control, and "they facilitate a transformation of consciousness and encourage an attitude of compassion . . . Each traveler through the Interlife can obtain exactly what is appropriate for his stage of growth."

So, as in this life, we see what we believe. If you are a fundamentalist Christian and you believe in purgatory, when you first start your Interlife journey, you may well see fire and brimstone. And so it goes until you reach the upper levels of vibration and come into your true essence, leaving any vestige of your body/mind behind. Others may find themselves at the right hand of Jesus or the Buddha, or in their grandmother's arms. In *Life Between Life* (1986), Whitton describes the journey thus: "Those who have reported personal observations of a life between life can be compared to the mariners of old who returned from a long voyage south with an absurd tale of the sun shining from the north . . . To venture into the unknown is often to savor experiences that confound contemporary wisdom."

Recorded History

The recorded research around Interlife journeys is comparatively recent. But the journeying itself has been recorded for thousands of years.

Although it is believed that the early Egyptians were the first to teach the concept of the soul's being immortal, the Greek philosopher Pythagoras brought the concept into full fruition when he taught it as if it were his own.

Pre-Columbian civilizations like the Aztecs, Mayans, and Toltecs (2000 BCE–1400 AD) believed in the Interlife. Egyptian mythology (2500 BCE) also strongly considered the Interlife as part of existing life and religion — hence the packing of pets, wives, mistresses, and other worldly goods into tombs along with the interred bodies. Currently, and since they began hundreds of years before the time of Christ, both the Hindu and Buddhist religions also believe in the Interlife, or Bardo.

The Interlife, the space or corridor between incarnations, is the time we are given to consider our karmic destiny and make the choices that will best fulfill that destiny. In *Life Between Life*, Whitton observes how

> [i]n the between-life state the soul reviews its performance across many lifetimes and chooses to resolve or atone for certain deeds in the next life. While past mistakes confront the soul in the bardo, most karmic adjustments can only be made by returning to physical

existence and reencountering, in many instances, those with whom the karma has been established.

The Tibetans have always been aware of this and still hold sacred the *Tibetan Book of the Dead*, written by the great master Padma Sambhava in the eighth or ninth century, as a guide to the journey between lifetimes.

The Tibetan description of the Interlife differs in many ways from the contemporary version of life between lives. For instance, it doesn't contain a council for the life review. Nor does the more ancient version include the element of conscious learning. We are, in the modern day, more conscious of the ability to make specific choices around the journey of our lives.

For centuries, Aboriginal shamanistic journeys often passed through a form of Interlife as they made their way through the passages of soul lifetimes, taking on the form of plants or animals to gather wisdom from a different point of view and sometimes completely physically shape-shifting while on the journey.

In all cases, the Interlife is seen as a place of peace and rest as well as a place of learning before the soul evolves into a different state of consciousness and reincarnates or moves to a higher realm.

The Goal of the Interlife

During our time in the Interlife, we learn that the ultimate goal on the physical plane—the here and now—is to know ourselves. During each of our lifetimes, we are offered many lessons. Some of these are painful, but all challenge us to know who we are. Painful childhood: do we succumb to the victimization of it or, through help, learn to move forward into peaceful adulthood? Destructive relationships, at work, at home, in the family: do we stay there as victims or make the choice to change the situation? Do we see hunger, disease, and fear in others and walk away, or do we do what we can to make a difference? These are the choices we make about our own souls' journey and growth—in each lifetime.

However, we also learn that our experiences are given to us by ourselves. We choose what is to be experienced in the life, so that we can learn the lessons we need to learn.

Our journey through the Interlife is a time for reflection and learning. We are here to make important decisions, and the more we understand about our life lessons, the better prepared we will be to learn from them and to know who we really are. "Your ultimate power lies in the fact that you can leave any situation that is not to your liking," Leonard Jacobson states in *Journey into Now* (2007). "You can leave for a few minutes, you can leave for a few hours, or you can leave for good. This means that you never have to be a victim again."

> *I see the potential for a new world being born in front of me and all around me, and I feel the only way to bring that potential into being is to know myself.*
>
> — GARY ZUKAV

Consider This:

- What do you feel and think about the "corridors in between" in your current life?

- What have you learned from them?

Chapter 9

Heaven and Hell on Earth

To different minds, the same world is a hell, and a heaven.

—Ralph Waldo Emerson

Hell on earth is a given right now. Practically everywhere you look, you can see evidence of the ghastly state into which so much of the world has sunk. And so it has been for a while.

Ask anyone who has been through the Holocaust about hell on earth, or survivors of the Bosnian war, or Darfur. Ask the starving in Bangladesh. Look at the children who are brutally abused by their own parents, or the women who are routinely and ritually mutilated. Look at the cruelty to animals that is beyond understanding; or the lowest, deepest forms of depression; or the mindless, psychotic destruction of life. Surely these must count as hell on earth.

Heaven on earth is also a given right now. When we see the sun come up over a mountain, or set and dip below a peaceful ocean, we exhale: "This is heaven." When I mountain-trekked in the Adirondacks, I'd turn a corner on the path and see before me mountains stacked up, one behind the other, covered in grasses and flowers of colors not seen at sea level; hawks and eagles circling overhead; the sky, clear, bright, vivid blue; ancient rocks sharing their solid-state energy and the sound of quiet. Silence. Peace and beauty. Heaven on earth. For me. At that time. I still remember it in my heart-mind.

The blossoming of trees and flowers each spring. The giggle of little girls. A crying, ongoing belly laugh with my sister and friends. The purr of a cat on a lap, or the wet nose of a dog in the hand. Eyes that welcome with love. Each morning I awake healthy, with a new day to enjoy. This is my heaven!

> *In the final analysis the hope of every person is simply peace of mind.*
> —THE DALAI LAMA

I have often wondered if, in fact, our Interlife, as our heaven and hell, is right here, right now, at this time, on this planet.

Interlife on Earth

Isn't all of life a series of little deaths and rebirths? We are all constantly in a state of flux. In the first chapter, I talked about how our bodies are forever changing—being born and dying at a cellular level. In addition, part of me believes that, during times of great introspection, we are, in fact, in Bardo. Think about it. When do the most profound spiritual changes take place in our lives?

During a "dark night of the soul," there is nowhere to go but toward the light. Our spirits are at their most vulnerable. Everything is stripped away, and we are naked in the face of our weaknesses. The very nature of a rock-bottom moment, such as the turning point for an alcoholic or drug addict, is that we finally realize how far we have fallen and how far we have to go. There is so much pain, withdrawal, and searching for truth. The yearning has a fierce power. We know that we have a lesson—perhaps many lessons—that we have to learn. Could this condition be Bardo?

Bardo, or the Interlife, is the place we go between lives to refuel, refocus, heal, and redirect our spiritual growth. We come out of it when we are reborn into fresh new lives—lives pregnant with possibilities for healing and evolution.

Life is a process of becoming, a combination of states we have to go through. Where people fail is that they wish to elect a state and remain in it. This is a kind of death.

—ANAÏS NIN

Isn't this exactly what happens when we reach the deepest depths of depression or depravity or desperation? There is nowhere to go but up, and the process of coming out of such a state brings the opportunity for innumerable spiritual lessons. This is the very definition of a soul's rebirth. It is the time of life lessons, the time for planning future growth, the time for the soul's shift back into the light.

This is the equivalent of the Interlife journey. Our souls are wiped clean and have the chance to start over.

We see it many times in classical literature and in history—the rebirthing of the human soul into another manifestation after a tragedy.

Dante and the Interlife

One famous and superb example of this theme can be found in Dante's *Inferno*, written in 14th-century Italy. *The Inferno*, Italian for "hell," is the first part of the epic poem *The Divine Comedy*, which depicts Dante's allegorical journey through the underworld. It is a story that unfolds on two levels—one literal, where the actions and images are taken at face value, and the other purely symbolic, where all the major details actually represent something else, something bigger.

From the first scene of *The Inferno*, the poem is rich with symbolism. The story opens on the evening of Good Friday. As Dante is following a dark path through the forest, he loses his way.

> Midway in our life's journey, I went astray from the
> straight road and woke to find myself alone in a
> dark wood.

Dante can see the sun through the tops of the trees and tries to find his way out of the woods, but his path is blocked by three beasts. He retreats back into the forest full of fear.

A dark path, a lost traveler, obstacles blocking his way to the light. Do you see a theme developing here?

Dante meets a guide—the ghost of Virgil, the great Roman poet—who has come to help him find his way. Virgil tells him that they will have to travel through hell in order to get to heaven.

Again, the theme.

Virgil leads Dante into hell, where he witnesses tortured souls who are trapped in a sort of pre-limbo, being chased and bitten by hornets for all of eternity.

According to Dante, hell is organized into nine circles, each housing sinners who committed progressively worse crimes. The first circle, for example, is for pagans who never knew Christ—a relatively minor sin. The next seven circles house souls who "specialized" in one of the seven deadly sins. The ninth circle is for the most depraved souls of all—betrayers of trust: "Abandon hope, all ye who enter here."

Dante goes through all eight circles and comes to the ninth, where he finds himself in the absolute lowest region of hell—an icy lake in which sinners stand frozen. Dante observes several sub-circles inside the ninth circle and then sees a huge shadowy figure before him. It is Lucifer himself, waist-deep in ice. Virgil and Dante have to climb down Lucifer's massive form in order to get out of hell. They emerge on Easter morning just before sunrise.

Again the theme! Dante has to reach the deepest pits of hell, even touch the devil himself, in order to cross into sunlight. Even better, he emerges on Easter Sunday, a holiday that, for Christians like Dante, celebrates resurrection and new life. Does this sound like the quintessential dark-night-of-the-soul journey?

The symbolism is clear: Sometimes you have to reach the very bottom, the worst possible place, before you can emerge cleansed and victorious. This theme is embodied in the last lines of the poem:

> To get back up to the shining world from there
> My guide and I went into that hidden tunnel . . .
> Where we came forth, and once more saw the stars.

This theme of symbolic death and rebirth has been written and recorded in Western culture since well before the 14th century. In 800 BCE, Homer wrote the classical Greek epic *The Odyssey*, in which the hero, Odysseus, undergoes several symbolic deaths and rebirths in his spiritual voyage toward enlightenment.

More recently, movies have picked up the theme. In *Revenge of the Sith, Part III* of the Star Wars saga, the themes of birth, death, and rebirth are interwoven—Padmé's life ends as her children, Luke and Leia, are born and Anakin is subsumed into Darth Vader. The end of one cycle (the death of the Republic) leads to the beginning of another (the birth of the Empire). Terry Gilliam's 1991 film *The Fisher King*, with Robin Williams and Jeff Bridges, has Bridges' character descend into the hell of an emotional breakdown before he can redeem (and resurrect) himself by helping the character

> *You and I are essentially infinite choice-makers. In every moment of our existence, we are in that field of all possibilities where we have access to an infinity of choices.*
>
> —DEEPAK CHOPRA

played by Robin Williams find love again after the devastating death of his wife.

The important point to take from this theme is that we have the power to transform our lives in the here and now. We can bring ourselves out of hell and into the light again. This is the exact goal of the Interlife, animated on earth.

If each of us is living in the Interlife right now, what do we do with that information? If the point of the Interlife is to encourage and prompt spiritual growth, and the Interlife is right now, how do we approach that challenge?

It comes down to creating your own heaven or hell — creating your own Interlife.

The Power of Perspective

You are walking through the park one morning and come upon a young couple having a breakfast picnic. They are lost in their own world, canoodling and kissing in the grass.

Just before your walk, your partner blew up at you for leaving a towel on the bathroom floor. You are still seething with repressed anger and resentment. There's a part of you that feels as though your relationship is disintegrating.

So, coming across this young couple when you are in that state of mind, your immediate reaction is one of dismissal. "Get a room," you think. Or, you silently smirk at the thought that, in a relatively short amount of time, their blissful union will probably end.

On the other hand, maybe you're taking this walk to work after a breakfast made lovingly for you by your partner, who still adores you after many years together.

So when you come across the young couple, you think: "How wonderful to be young and in love. They have so much to look forward to." You finish your walk with a spring in your step and a smile on your face, thinking of your partner at home.

We see what we are looking for—always and in all ways.

In other words, your experience on earth is entirely up to you. The things that happen to you may be random, but the way you react is fully in your power. And it is your reaction to life that determines whether you walk every day in heaven or in hell.

Choosing Heaven

Heaven is all about the state of mind you choose. There is nothing inherently wrong with reacting to life's challenges in anger, fear, or sadness. Those are natural human emotions. But dwelling in these negative energies does nothing but attract more negativity. We all know people who see themselves as victims—accident-prone, always attracting the wrong lover, always catching a cold, or always living in the past in their less-than-ideal early lives.

All this does is perpetuate a negative state of mind.

The key to owning your perspective lies in your ability to center yourself and connect to your natural sense of peace and balance. If you are able, at any given moment, to "shake it off"—whatever "it" is—and let go of the old and move forward into the peace within yourself, you will be creating an oasis inside of you where only goodness can dwell. "Love is what we were born with," Marianne Williamson argues in

A Return to Love (1996). "Fear is what we have learned here. The spiritual journey is the relinquishment—or unlearning—of fear and the acceptance of love back into our hearts."

The inner silence that comes from this acceptance allows you to tune in to that still, small voice that lives in each of us. This voice guides and balances you. It is the voice of your higher self, of Spirit, of God—however you choose to name it. When you are able to hear this voice, you can see clearly. You can make the right decisions for you. You can follow your heart. Even more than that, you can see each moment of life for the beauty and majesty it contains. This is the definition of heaven on earth.

Mastering the ability to hear the voice is paradoxically the easiest and most difficult thing you can undertake.

> *The mind is its own place,*
> *and in itself*
> *Can make a heaven of hell, a*
> *hell of heaven.*
>
> —JOHN MILTON, PARADISE LOST

The voice is eternal and pervasive; it is always with you. But it is easy to get lost in the dust and noise of your—guilt—anger—resentment—shame—which can get in the way. Learning to slough away this negativity takes conscious choice and dedication. Also, sometimes, professional help. And often, when you're cruising smoothly along with your new, peaceful, heavenly soul, you think you've done all the spiritual work you'll ever need to do. Then something happens that plunges you right back to where you started and you think you never learned anything to begin with! It happens to us all.

When I'm training people to be better public speakers or presenters, they can see themselves improving with each session—and then they may fall into the pit of despair! For some reason, nothing works the way it should; techniques are forgotten; thoughts disappear; and they are overcome by feelings of helplessness and hopelessness. This is when I explain to them that it is the same process for anyone who is trying to learn something new—athletes, performers, speakers, and spiritual seekers. We all reach a plateau and need a kick-start to get to the next level.

> *The universe is transformation; our life is what our thoughts make it.*
>
> —MARCUS AURELIUS

Achieving heaven on earth is an ongoing process. It takes constant work and dedication. Like weight loss, you can't just stop once you reach your goal. Otherwise, you'll backslide. Spiritual peace requires regular maintenance, because there will always be factors that seem to prey on that peace. It's a continuous series of decisions.

When you finally choose this path, you will be living out the goal of the Interlife. If you choose to walk in peace and see each "problem" as an opportunity for healing, you will be living in the ideal state. You will be creating your own good karma—creating your own heaven on earth.

Heaven on Earth in Every Moment

We can experience heaven on earth as being here and now, in this moment and in successive moments of Now. Yesterday morning, I was out walking and I suddenly stopped and became present to and aware of everything. I was fully in the here and now. "We have to try to get rid of the notion of time," Paolo Coelho warns (*The Alchemist*, 1993). "And when you have an intense contact of love with nature or another human being, like a spark, then you understand that there is no time and that everything is eternal."

Each of us has the ability simply to stop and be here and now in each and every moment. Why don't you just do that right now? Stop reading this. Look up and out into the world. Be present.

Notice the sounds, the smells; observe what's around you, your thoughts, your emotions. Be aware of being aware. You can do this at any time under any circumstances.

Make your heaven on earth, where you are, right now . . . always.

Exploring Your Own Interlife

Ready to take the plunge—or should I say flight—into your own Interlife? If possible, it's advisable to find a reputable, experienced Interlife facilitator, but if there isn't one in your area, or you can't wait—you want it now—then I'm happy to provide you with this safe, gentle meditation/hypnosis script that will enable you to experience the process. A few caveats:

- If you are doing this without a professional facilitator, find a trusted friend to read the script to you, or

- Record this meditation yourself, so that you can play it back at a time that is appropriate for you.

- Choose a time and place where you can relax and not be disturbed by the telephone, children, or dog!

- Try not to be too self-critical along the way—just allow.

The good news about doing this for yourself is that you don't have to wait for someone else's schedule to fit in with yours. The not-so-good news is that you will not be able to relax completely because some part of your conscious mind will need to be active to keep you feeling safe and on-track.

Notes on reading the script—either for yourself or your friend:

- Take your time with it. Speak slowly, probably slower than you normally do.

- Where there are dots (. . .), take extra time for your subconscious mind to process.

- When you are actively in the Interlife, meeting your soul circle and others, allow extra time, because this is the purpose of the journey—to interact and learn from those you meet. Honor this time, and allow it to process fully before moving on to the next section.

Soul Circle Meditation Script
For Self-Recording

Find somewhere to sit and relax in quiet. Take a few deep breaths to ready yourself for your journey. Focus on your body and do what you need to do to make yourself comfortable. Close your eyes and notice your breath . . . as it flows in and out. Feel the coolness as it flows in . . . and the warmth as it flows out. Allow yourself to feel more and more relaxed with each out breath . . . flowing in and flowing out . . . flowing in and flowing out . . . the coolness of the inflow . . . and the warm outflow.

Re-arrange your arms and legs as comfortably as you can. Focus on your breath . . . the warm outflow of each breath takes you deeper . . . and deeper . . . and deeper . . . gently breathing, never-ending, the cycle of breath . . . flowing easily and gently.

Take a moment now and go inside yourself to find the source of your breath . . . take a moment and honor that part of you . . . the part that allows and monitors your breath, allowing your brain to function with oxygen and your heart to continue its life-affirming rhythm.

Go inside to find your pulse, the beat of your heart, and notice how it has slowed down . . . how it has relaxed along with your mind . . . as you follow your breath . . . Now take a moment . . . and thank and bless that part of you . . . your heart . . . that allows you to live and love and take part in the world at this time.

Now take a deep breath . . . let it out . . . and go still deeper into a place of deep relaxation, where you are aware but completely relaxed. As you imagine being in the most wonderful place . . . a safe place, a place where you feel most relaxed . . . a place where you feel the most good . . . imagine how it looks . . . Is it inside or outside?

And as you picture or think about what it is like . . . notice how your body is becoming more and more relaxed with every out breath . . . the warmth of the out breath takes you deeper . . . and deeper into relaxation . . . as you see yourself now . . . sense yourself now . . . in this wonderful place where you feel the best . . . the most relaxed . . . the most safe . . .

Maybe it's a beach . . . maybe it's a comfortable chair in your home . . . maybe it's the dock at the cottage . . . Whatever it is . . . it is your safe place . . . just see it in your mind . . . and feel the relaxation it brings in your body . . . You may even notice some sounds associated with this place . . . birds singing, or water trickling . . . or the sound of leaves rustling in the breeze . . . or there may just be a very peaceful silence . . . and each breath takes you deeper . . . and deeper into relaxation . . . every out breath takes you deeper . . . and deeper . . .

As you imagine yourself relaxing in your safe, wonderful place . . . maybe feeling the warmth of the sun on your skin . . . if you're on a beach . . . or the comforting feeling of being in familiar sur- roundings . . . if you're in a favorite chair at home . . . whatever is right for you . . . is right for you . . . it allows you to relax so com- pletely . . . and more completely than you have relaxed in a long . . . long time . . . with every breath going deeper and deeper into relaxation . . .

And as you continue relaxing now . . . your mind is opening to the awareness of a powerful healing spirit within you . . . during this time . . . this session . . . your subconscious mind will only accept suggestions that are totally safe and in line with the highest good of your entire being . . . Any suggestions you accept will function in the ideal time frame and in the safest and most comfortable ways. If, in the future, any of the suggestions become outdated, or fail to serve your highest good . . . they will automatically dissipate and disappear from your mind.

Letting go . . . now . . . even more, with every breath, noticing that every third out breath doubles your relaxation . . . it happens . . . easily, automatically, without any thought on your part . . . easily . . . effortlessly . . .

Imagine a flight of stairs, a beautiful golden staircase leading you into the deepest state of relaxation. As I count down from 1 to 10, allow yourself to drift down these stairs, lightly and gently with each breath, drifting down . . . deeper . . . 1 . . . 2 . . . deeper and deeper . . . 3 . . . 4 . . . moving down into a deep state of relaxation, where nothing bothers you, nothing disturbs you, going down . . . 5 . . . 6 . . . letting go . . . the deeper you go, the better you feel . . . 7 . . . 8 . . . all the way down now . . . 9 . . . and 10 . . . deeper and deeper.

If you so choose, you may ask that your higher power be present to guide and protect you during this program . . . and throughout the mind-body balancing.

As your body relaxes, you may begin to feel pleasantly blurry and distant . . . As you relax more . . . and more . . . you may allow yourself to connect into the helpful flow of the universe . . . the ebb and flow of the water . . . the clouds passing by . . . and perhaps even the warmth of the sun. That's right . . . in this beautiful relaxed state, you can connect into the power and beauty of the universe.

In a moment—but not right now—I will ask you to lend me your imagination and go to your favorite place . . . see and feel how wonderful it is . . . how peaceful and calm . . . the more you focus on where you are and the colors and textures, the smells and sounds . . . the deeper into relaxation you go.

So now . . . for a short while that seems like a long while . . . focus on what you can smell in your wonderful space . . . breathe in . . . gently but deeply now . . . the faint fragrance of flowers perhaps . . . or the sea . . .

And now . . . if you listen very carefully, what sounds can you hear? . . . Maybe the sound of birds . . . or music in the distance . . . or even water, trickling and soothing to your ears . . .

And look very carefully at what you can see . . . or imagine that you can see . . . look at the colors . . . notice how the light falls on the colors . . . notice the textures . . . maybe you want to reach out and touch the textures to feel the differences under your fingertips . . .

Letting go all of your day-to-day concerns . . . just relaxing down . . . following your . . . breathing . . . notice how smoothly and freely your breath is flowing . . . smoothly . . . freely . . . flowing breath . . . bringing oxygen down to your lungs . . . smoothly and freely . . . your breath flows . . .

Now . . . as your breath flows easily and smoothly . . . allow your mind to access your deep, healing wisdom . . .

Now imagine, if you will, in this beautiful, wonderful safe place, a magic line that allows you to journey back through time and space. This line is like a moving highway, and when you choose to step onto it, it will carry you back . . . back . . . through time and space, very quickly through months and years of your current life, into the womb of your mother . . . that dark warm place where you can feel the heartbeat. Rest there for a moment, and feel the heartbeat of your mother, surrounding you, healing you, connecting you to all there is where you are right now . . . feeling safe and protected.

And as you move, feeling pulled or floating safely . . . floating and moving . . . you may see a light . . . a bright white light or a cluster of lights . . . waiting to greet you on your journey. Take your time and move toward the light. It may be your primary guide or your group of guides. Just notice what you sense or feel or see.

How does this welcome being manifest itself for you? Is it someone you recognize? Does it have the shape of what we call a human being? Is it male or female, or does it exists for you as light or energy, waiting with love to greet you?

Notice how you are greeted. Are you surrounded by the energy of love, or does your guide move toward you, arms outstretched to welcome you? Just relax, note and enjoy the pleasure of this greeting . . . Notice the color of your guide's aura . . . and ask, if it is appropriate for you, that your guide give you his or her name.

Now ask your guide to tell you your soul color . . . and listen with your heart for the answer.

Ask, if it is appropriate for you, to know your soul name . . . that name which has traveled with you since time began . . . ask now for your soul name . . . and listen with your heart.

When you are ready, your guide will take you to meet the souls in your soul circle . . . those souls with whom you have made agreements and contracts to play out different lives with you at certain times, different lives to fulfill agreements—contracts and karmic agreements—even those that caused you pain, as these souls lived that life with you and for you, so that you could experience the lessons you needed to learn at that time, and maybe still do.

These souls who help you on your journey are your true soul mates, soul mates who come in and out of your lifetimes, over eons of time, to teach, to learn, to share, and to love. Your soul mates.

So journey now on this exciting path to meet your soul mates, your true partners in the soul journey.

Notice where your guide is taking you . . . and how you get there. Are you floating? Are you being pulled or do you suddenly appear somewhere with your soul circle waiting for you? . . .

Arrive now at the place of your soul circle . . . notice how you arrive and what you see there . . . I will take the time to give you the space to experience all you need to experience on this journey.

Notice how your soul group shows itself to you. Do they take on human form, or are they lights moving around singly, in pairs, or in clusters? Just notice what you perceive . . . maybe you see them and maybe you don't. Maybe you just KNOW that they are there . . . but however you receive this information, take note of it . . . now . . . Are they in a circle? In a line in front of you? Or all bunched up?

As you come toward them, are you in the center? . . . Or do you join together as one large cluster of brightness? Notice how it feels to be surrounded by those you travel with through time and space, through many lifetimes . . . notice how you are received, how they greet you.

How many of them can you sense or see?

As you get used to being with them and feeling your place with them . . . notice which one comes forward first to greet you . . . Is it a male or female energy? . . . Is this person in your life today in any form? . . . Have you shared other lifetimes with this person? . . . What is this soul's immortal name?

What role does this soul have in your life today—or in your soul growth? . . . Does it offer balance? Or show you kindness and generosity of spirit? . . . Does it bring you experience of hardship so you may learn? . . . Just be aware of your link to and relationship with this soul.

Now look around at the other souls in your group. With whom have you been incarnated most often in your past lives? . . . Who is in your life today? . . . What roles do they play in your life today?

Notice what feelings and thoughts you are receiving from your group.

Ask them to give you some messages that you may bring back with you to enhance your current life . . . just nod your head when you have received the messages.

Thank them and bid them farewell for a short while, which may seem like a long while. They remind you that you are—in truth—together all of the time . . . Separation doesn't exist.

Notice that certain phrases emerge from your heart that express what you wish most deeply for yourself—not just for today, but in an enduring way . . . Phrases that are big enough and general enough that you can ultimately wish them for all of your current life, for your loved ones . . . for all beings everywhere . . . You hear the murmuring . . .

"May I live in safety. May I be happy. May I be healthy. May I live with ease." . . . You gently repeat these phrases over and over as you journey back through the galaxy, back through the vibration of what we know as time . . . All people, all animals, all creatures, all those in existence, near and far . . . known to us and unknown to us . . . All beings on the earth . . . in the air . . . in the water. Those being born, those dying.

You feel the energy of this aspiration extending infinitely in front of you . . . to either side . . . behind you . . . above and below. As your heart extends in a boundless way, leaving no one out . . . may all beings live in safety, be happy, be healthy, live with ease.

Slowly and easily, you are being guided back to what we call the present time . . . Slowly changing your vibration, coming back now . . . to the present time . . . on this planet earth, at this present day.

As you enter the here and now . . . in a moment . . . I will count from 10 to 1 and you will return to full awareness, feeling grounded, alert, and ready for the life you live today.

10, 9, 8, 7. . . move your fingers and feet . . . 6, 5, 4 . . . shrug your shoulders . . . 3, 2, 1 . . .

Fully awake now.

May you live in safety. Be happy; be healthy; live with ease.

Consider This:

- By and large, which do you choose in your current life—heaven or hell?

- Which road do you take: the one that leads to pleasure, or the victim route of eternal emotional pain?

- Why do you choose this path?

Chapter 10

Using the Wisdom Learned

They always say that time changes things,
but you actually have to change them yourself.

— ANDY WARHOL

So you've done a past-life or Interlife regression. You've returned to your normal life, giddy with (your) new awareness.
You've had some revelations. You may have cracked the code
to personal mysteries that have haunted you for years. You've
had contact with the spirit world, and you have come away
from it feeling cleansed, rejuvenated, and blessed. These
kinds of feelings are impossible to ignore. So now what?

In my clinic, when I move clients into a past-life or Interlife regression, I can facilitate extraordinary therapeutic
interventions that often make radical changes within the clients: letting go of anger, toxic memories, or fear of living life
to the fullest.

One of the biggest challenges and potential drawbacks of
making positive personal changes is weaving those changes

smoothly into the fabric of everyday life. It's not always easy to live out the new insights gained during a major spiritual experience. You may have no idea even where to begin changing your own life. Or you may find that taking the initial steps to institute the changes is the easy part, but that getting those changes to stick can be much more difficult.

Either way, you are dealing with significant upheaval. If we build on the premise that most people view change as a difficult and frightening path into the unknown, we know we have lots of work to do. "Learn wisdom from the ways of a seedling," Stephen Sigmund advises us. "A seedling which is never hardened-off through stressful situations will never become a strong productive plant" (*Organic Gardening, Vol 31*, 1984).

Plunging headfirst into the unknown of change requires faith—and a plan. This chapter will offer you a plan for integrating your new knowledge smoothly into your life. All you have to do is bring the faith!

Introducing Your New Self

When people experience sudden positive change, a couple of things can happen. One is that, because you are happy about the change, you want everyone around you to be the same and do the same. You may become very eager to share your lessons with everyone you know and everyone you meet.

The people around you can respond to this in one of two ways. They either buy in and become supportive, trying to understand, accept, and even learn from this new person that is you. Or they feel resentful and try to diminish the benefits.

They may even make aggressive attempts to belittle your efforts and their benefits by making fun or using insults, or they may simply and flatly ignore any attempts you make to discuss the changes.

This kind of dynamic causes all sorts of problems. You may feel like an outsider, unable to relate to the people closest to you. Or you may feel hurt that others are so quick to dismiss what feels so important and life-changing to you. Their resistance, however, is to their detriment, not yours. As Tyron Edwards notes: "He that never changes his opinions, never corrects his mistakes, will never be wiser on the morrow than he is today."

People may be completely annoyed with your new self. They may feel as if you're on a spiritual high horse, or that you've turned self-righteous. You may come across as judgmental and above it all. This can rub the people close to you the wrong way. I've seen how people react when a family member successfully loses excess weight or quits smoking. They are not always loving and supportive—especially if the client emerges with a "holier than thou" attitude, expecting others to eat smaller portions, give up smoking, and start exercising!

One way to avoid this is just to sit with your new knowledge for a while. Absorb the new energies you have created for yourself. Then follow the plan outlined in this chapter, and slowly start making the changes. The folks you care about will notice the changes, and may well learn from your doing, not your talking about the doing.

Clearly, integrating the positive personal changes gleaned from an Interlife awakening is a delicate process. If you are to take the learnings and information from the Interlife into your current life, you need to have the understanding and tools to integrate this new knowledge. You need to be secure within your "newness."

This self-security helps you feel more comfortable; it also helps you integrate new wisdom in such a way as not to cause discomfort to those around you. Remember, it's not uncommon for friends and loved ones to resent change. So it is important that you have the tools to integrate the changes seamlessly.

> *The personal life deeply lived always expands into truths beyond itself.*
>
> — ANAÏS NIN

An additional role for your facilitator or regression therapist is to enable you to absorb the new into the old slowly and to help you let go of any outdated or non-useful ideas, patterns, people, or processes.

You do this through the Absorption Process, which I have developed and used with many of my Interlife or life-between-lives clients.

The Absorption Process

The Absorption Process is designed to help you integrate your Interlife journey into your regular life smoothly. It will help you identify and clarify the lessons learned, adjust to the changes that are happening and how they may affect your life and the people around you, and learn how to deal with those effects.

The process breaks down into three steps that can be accomplished in three parts, with homework in between. Your Interlife facilitator may have a similar process through which to guide you. If not, you can use my easy-to-follow protocols on your own.

Integration Protocol Step One— The New and the Old

To start, you need to make two lists.

List One

This list should contain all of the thoughts, feelings, understandings, people, and wisdom you gained from the Interlife journey that you wish to take with you into your powerfully rich future.

The list breaks down into three sections:

- The people and places you want with you in your future—be selective here and choose people who help you feel good about yourself

- The thoughts and understandings that will carry you into your future

- The actions, habits, and processes that will enable you to move into your future—what you're actually going to do to move your life forward.

The list should come from what you learned during your Interlife journey.

List Two

This list should contain all the people, places, thoughts, understandings, actions, habits, and processes of your current life that can get in the way of your growth in this lifetime.

You may find that people or patterns you held dear in your life before your journey no longer fit the new self you have embraced—people who rain on your parade, or who are Negative Nellies, or who are (intentionally or unintentionally) discouraging, unsupportive, or insulting. You may choose to leave these people behind as you move forward. Or you may choose to try to find ways to integrate the new you into life with these people so that you don't totally lose them, but rather learn to manage and lessen their impact on you. Members of your family, for instance.

Either way, making a list of these people or habits or patterns before the issues arise will help prepare you for these challenges and make you better able to handle them.

Homework One—Write It Down!
Just Thinking It Isn't Enough

Write a journal entry based around the idea of "My New Self." Answer the following questions and any others that come up that you want to explore:

- Who I am today? Who am I in the future?

- What are some of the most noticeable positive changes I feel starting to happen in my life because of my new self?

- How do I feel about these changes?

- What obstacles do I anticipate I may encounter as I'm trying to accommodate the changes?

- How do I sense those around me feel about the changes?

- How will I present my new self to the world to allow those in my world to buy into and support my change?

Integration Protocol Step Two—The Plan

In this session, you'll be using the previous homework and refining the description of your new self. You need practical ways to integrate the changes taking place. Designing a plan of action helps you move forward with new awareness and new perspective.

Look back at the changes you wrote about in the previous session, as well as the obstacles you anticipated.

Use the following exercise to identify specific things you can do in your everyday life that will help introduce the changes and help people in your inner circle accept or, at least, accommodate them.

The top three things I want to change in my life are:

1. _____

2. _____

3. _____

The three things I will do differently every day in my family life are:

1. _____

2. _____

3. _____

The three things I will do differently every day in my work life are:

1. _____

2. _____

3. _____

The three things I will do differently every day in my personal life are:

1. _____

2. _____

3. _____

My first four steps to achieve this new action plan are:

1. _____

I will achieve this step by this time: _____

2. _____

I will achieve this step by this time: _____

3. _____

I will achieve this step by this time: _____

4. _____

I will achieve this step by this time: _____

Homework Two — Selling Your New Self

Start to "sell" your new self to the outside world by taking at least one step of the action plan. You may like to write a journal entry about your experiences while enacting the plan, answering the following questions:

- What step of my action plan did I choose to take first? Why did I choose this as my first step?

- What difficulties, if any, did I encounter in taking this step? How well did I handle them?

- What was the most gratifying part of this step? What validation did I receive—from another person, from myself, from the universe?

Integration Protocol Step Three—The Future

The purpose of this session is to give you the ability to carry out the remaining steps of your action plan, and then maintain that focus into the future.

Update and reassess how far you have come with your plan. Using the results of Homework Two, review the area of change you chose to approach first, the action taken, the difficulties faced, and the validations experienced.

If you have fears or concerns about completing the action plan, you can let go of them by identifying the difficulties you may face in the subsequent steps of your plan. You may even benefit from answering question number 2 from Homework Two—What difficulties did I encounter, and how did I handle them?—for each step of the plan. But instead of answering the question after completing the step, answer the question before completing the step, as a kind of preliminary "prep tool."

Just this little bit of further preparation can make a profound difference in your experience of instituting change. It offers many advantages, not the least of which is the confidence that comes from feeling ready for whatever may occur.

Another advantage of having a well-thought-out plan for action is that you will be more capable of repairing any damage that may come into your relationships. When a difficulty arises, you won't be caught off-guard and freeze. You'll know what to do to heal or manage the situation.

This is the time to use self-hypnosis or meditation to confirm the changes in your subconscious mind. I have made a self-hypnosis CD for people who aren't sure about the practice of self-hypnosis; you can work your plan with that if you like. Once you've learned the technique, that ability will stay with you for the rest of your life. A gift to yourself!

In addition, at the end of this chapter is a script to help you visualize your new future and to see the steps you need to take to get yourself there. For the best results, you should record this script and play it to yourself at least once a day for twenty-one days, as it takes twenty-one days to make or break a habit. This script, along with learning self-hypnosis, will enable you to re-charge your own batteries any time you find your energy and focus waning.

The Interlife journey reveals profound, life-altering lessons. You return from these journeys filled with joy and wonder and enthusiasm over the new revelations. You'll probably be eager to integrate the revelations into your life, but change like this is never easy. It's a delicate process. It's easy to make mistakes that can alienate you from people you care about. If this happens, the temptation to abandon the changes can be strong.

> *. . . the moment one definitely commits oneself, then Providence moves too. All sorts of things occur to help one that would never otherwise have occurred.*
>
> —GOETHE

It would be a big shame to waste the deep and far-reaching experience of the Interlife simply because you don't have the tools to bridge the gap between the spiritual world and the concrete. This chapter is your tool. Use it well and with joy, because it is the start of a new you! And you can never un-know that!

Visualizing the New You

Here is a self-hypnosis script for you to record and listen to, at least once a day for twenty-one days.

Do what you need to do to relax completely. Turn off the phone. Close the door on pets, children, or any other potential interrupters. And allow yourself the following moments of peace—no one wanting anything from you; no one needing anything from you. This time is for you.

Just relax, take a deep breath and close your eyes, and follow your breathing. Notice the coolness of the in-breath and the warmth of the out-breath, and allow yourself to drift and float, easily . . . just following your breath . . . relaxing . . . down . . .

Slowly, you become aware that you are not merely drifting aimlessly; you are moving toward a goal. The goal is yourself as you wish to be. Imagine yourself strong, confident, and relaxed—easily drawing abundance into your life and feeling good about yourself. All mental capabilities are growing sharper, clearer, and more effective with each passing day. Your body is in excellent physical condition, looking good, feeling good, vital and energized. You are in command of your body and your mind. You are drawing into your life an ever-growing abundance of peace, prosperity, health, love, and joy. You are spiritually aware and growing. You are able to do all those things that are important to you and do them well. Joyous in every area of your life.

You become aware of all the wonderful things that you now have available in your life—your own special blessings. Be aware of the abundance you now have, steadily growing with each breath you take. Be aware of people in your life who love you and those you love. Be aware of the possibilities and opportunities in your life now and those you are creating in your future.

With your new awareness, you make time for success and joy in every area of your life—spiritual, physical, emotional, and mental. This word "success" refers to the goals you have set that empower you in every area of your life. Success is emotional balance, joyous fulfilling relationships, physical health and fitness, spiritual growth, and an ever-deeper consciousness of your oneness with the universe and the forces of the universe.

You are now committing to create the life you want to lead, to be the person you want to become. See yourself; feel yourself there. Imagine yourself watching a very special movie. Your movie starts now and ends with you having accomplished all the goals—spiritual, mental, and physical—that you have set for yourself. Watch the movie of your new self as it becomes the new you. When you have seen your special movie through to the end, see it running again and again, each time brighter, more colorful, more detailed.

And bring that picture back with you as you slowly return to the here and now. Each time, bringing the energy of that movie back stronger and more intensely into your body, mind, and spirit—so that it becomes who you are today, on this planet, at this time.

Count back now to this time and place, and feel yourself become aware . . .

10, 9, 8, 7, 6 . . . feel your body come awake now . . . 5, 4, 3, 2, and 1. Wide awake. Clear, relaxed, and purposeful about your future.

Consider This:

- Who around you will be affected by your change?

- How will you handle that?

Chapter 11

Case Histories and Healings

Unless you walk out into the unknown, the odds of making a profound difference in your life are pretty low.

— TOM PETERS

The more work I do around the soul journey, the more I am amazed by it. I feel humbled and privileged to work with clients during their journeys. Every good facilitator I've worked with or trained feels the same way and comes to understand that they are only the facilitators. The clients' souls are the miraculous part of the process.

Most people undertake the journey into a past life because they are curious. They may have heard or read about past-life regression, or perhaps they have always felt a strong affinity for a particular place or time in history. Some have dreams that recur and that are very real to them.

Those who take the journey often come away with a better understanding about the connectedness of life, and about who they are and perhaps why they are that way. They need not be of a spiritual nature. In fact, many are downright cynical at the beginning. But most inevitably find themselves opening up to new possibilities and a clearer sense of purpose.

A number of themes or ideas emerge from past-life regression journeys. Whether the clients are looking for healing or wisdom or some kind of peace and understanding about where they are in their current lives, the "life lessons" that they bring back with them from past lives are usually clear and pertinent to the lives they are living today.

Following are some of the people (their names have been changed) who have experienced past-life regression at the clinic. Their lessons and the wisdom are universal.

Love

If you love everything, you will perceive the divine mystery in things. . . . I maintain that [hell] is the suffering of being unable to love.

—FYODOR DOSTOYEVSKY

Linda

First Life

Linda came into the clinic to understand why—in her words—she always chose "losers" to love and ended up being emotionally hurt and abandoned.

In her first life, Linda said she was a female, wearing dainty black shoes, a black dress, and black shawl. Her blonde hair was dirty and pinned up. She appeared to be in an older house with lots of stairs—a bar or saloon with lots of people, including cowboys dancing and being really loud. There were several girls wearing feathers and sequins. Her name was Jenny and she was twenty-six. At night, she slept in a single bed in a small room above the bar, with a rotted wood floor and a light bulb hanging from the ceiling. There appeared to be a man she cared about, but, at one point, she found herself in her room crying, with someone on the bed who had died of a heart attack.

She then saw herself outside the bar, where it was very quiet. The bar appeared to be closed for good and she was feeling very alone. She realized she would be leaving this place. She then found herself across from the saloon on a balcony, from which she jumped and died.

Wisdom

The wisdom Linda believed came from this life was: Be careful whom you love. She hadn't been allowed to love and, by choosing to go against that, loving had cost the person in her life. She realized that she needed to

The virtues we acquire, which develop slowly within us, are the invisible links that bind each one of our existences to the others—existences which the spirit alone remembers, for Matter has no memory for spiritual things.

—HONORÉ DE BALZAC

be more discriminating in her choice of men, and started working to understand what she really needed and wanted in a relationship.

Annette

First Life

Annette came into the clinic looking for the basis of her sense of resentment. Born into a very large family (she was the fifth of six children), she often felt overlooked and unheard—even as an adult. In regression, she found herself a twenty-year-old male with dark skin, in a place where the houses were small and people were working and digging. The men carried baskets on their shoulders. A king appeared in a procession and people began to cheer. The king had a big dark beard and wore a small gold crown. His wife sat in a chair behind him.

The man then found himself working with the king, making plans for a school to be built, from which he deduced that he must be quite important. As an old man, he was a teacher, teaching a large number of children. When he died, people came to his home to pray over him and, after his death, he was carried through the town and people were singing.

Wisdom

Annette believed the lesson of the life was to be kind to people and help them. The wisdom was that love is the most important thing—that we can overcome anything with love. It helped her take another look at the interaction of her family and to realize that love was there, but that she had been unaware of it.

Sandra

First Life

Sandra was searching for meaning in her life. She said she had always felt that a part of her was missing or not accessed. In her first life, Sandra was a male — a pilot in the British Air Force during wartime, flying a bomber and dropping bombs. He felt sadness, knowing he was killing innocent people. His reluctance to carry out his duty finally led him to crash his own plane to stop the killing. The lesson of this life, for Sandra, was to love and show this love to her children.

Second Life

In her second life, Sandra was a courtesan in 18th-century Europe, living a completely hedonistic life that included orgies. She gave detailed descriptions of the "goings on" and laughed as she recounted some of these antics. She died a quiet, peaceful death, surrounded by friends. The wisdom she gained from that life was to live for life, and to be bold and unafraid.

Wisdom

Despite the contrast between Sandra's two past lives, there was a love of life in both of them. One was forced to take life away and paid a high price for doing so; the other grabbed life and celebrated it. Sandra left the session feeling energized and "ready to take on the world."

Helen

The Lives

Helen came to the clinic suffering from anxiety and depression, hoping that past-life regression would help her. She was regressed through three past lives, each of which had a lesson to teach.

In the first, Helen had been in an arranged loveless marriage. Her life became so automatic that she felt less than human—just moving through her chores day by day, as she said. Sun-up to sundown was planned and predictable. She took from that life the understanding that she needed to be stronger emotionally, to take hold of each moment and live now.

In the second life, as part of a traveling tribe in the desert, Helen was betrothed to a boy when they were both five years old. When she reached puberty at about fourteen years of age, the wedding was arranged. During the ceremony, a raiding enemy band swept through the village and she and her husband were killed (scalped).

In Helen's third life, she came into the life as an adult woman whose face had been disfigured in a fire caused by her alcoholic father. Her elder brother looked after her for a while, but soon abandoned her. It was through the kindness of a religious man that she found a place to live and work in the service of a wealthy woman. She died in servitude and in peace.

Wisdom

Through each of these lives ran the recurring theme that love mattered more than anything else, and that love can come in many forms and from many sources.

Family

To put the world right in order, we must first put the nation in order; to put the nation in order, we must first put the family in order; to put the family in order, we must first cultivate our personal life; we must first set our hearts right.

— CONFUCIUS

Elizabeth

First Life

Elizabeth came for a past-life regression purely out of curiosity, wanting to find out if she could learn anything about her relationship with her mother—which was distant. She slipped into hypnosis and past life very easily and quickly and found herself outside, in the countryside, a twelve-year-old female with no shoes on. She was wearing an old dress with holes in it, but was surrounded by laughing children—two little boys and a girl. She saw her mother in a dark red dress and an apron, with her hair pinned up in a bun. The house they lived in was made of stone, and there were chickens in a shack attached to the house.

At some point some "scary guys" came into the house. Her mother screamed and one of the men yelled about something her father had done. The men hit her mother and grabbed her brother, taking him with them when they left. She saw her mother covered in blood, her face swollen.

Later in this lifetime, Elizabeth's mother became ill, and Elizabeth and her sister took care of her. Eventually, the mother died and the two girls wrapped her in a cloth and put her in the water, where she began to float away. She and her sister were alone and frightened, and Elizabeth went into the water and swam away, saying that she was "going to be with my mother." She saw her sister standing alone and crying.

Wisdom

Elizabeth was profoundly moved by the journey and unable to reconcile the depth of feelings she had during the session. She believes the wisdom from this life is that family is very important, so enjoy it.

Betty

First Life

Betty was a woman in her early twenties who had been drifting from job to job with no focus. She didn't know who she was or what she wanted from life. It took a while for her to access a past life and, when she did, she saw herself in Spain or Portugal as a middle-aged woman, near white sand and blue water. She was with her mother, on their last trip together before her mother became too old to travel. Betty knew she was part of a large, busy family with lots of children and cousins. They lived in the countryside, working hard and living off the land. Life was turbulent, because food on the table depended on the weather and the hard work of all the family members—some of whom didn't want to work hard at all. She died, still unmarried, but dependent on her family for their care-giving.

Wisdom

From this life, Betty brought back the lesson that happiness comes from hard work, sharing, and family. She left the clinic knowing that she needed to focus and find her way. She subsequently came back and took hypnosis sessions to help her set goals and achieve them.

Bob

First Life

Bob was a retired banker who was exploring his spirituality. He read extensively and felt he knew a great deal about regression work, but hadn't experienced it.

Bob's first past-life regression took him to a small village in the mountains. He was a male in his thirties wearing animal skins. He said he had lost his family to sickness and was very lonely. He seemed to be in Asia in the early 1500s.

In the next scene, he was in a town of some sort, where there were women on the streets and monks with bowls, but they didn't look at him. He felt invisible, unloved and unwanted. Someone brought him a bowl with rice, but he ate alone.

Eventually Bob found himself sick and in bed in a place where there were a lot of other sick, dying, and dead people around him. Someone took care of him, bathed and fed him; but there was no other treatment. He died alone and broken, his hopes and dreams shattered.

Wisdom

Bob was profoundly moved by his first regression and believed this life showed him the importance of family—that without family, there can be no home, no belonging.

The Power Is Within Us

Deep in their roots, all flowers keep the light.

—THEODORE ROETHKE

Joyce

First Life

Joyce was a Reiki practitioner and hypnotist who wanted to experience the journey herself. She entered a life as a barefoot male in a jungle, about twenty-five and surrounded by exotic birds. He was hunting for food with a bow and arrow, hoping to get a bird or animal for his family, which included his mother and sister.

Joyce then moved to a big celebration with drums, chanting, and dancing. Animals were being sacrificed in some sort of ritual. Joyce said later that she believed she was on an island, or possibly in Australia or New Zealand. She drew a picture of the body markings she had on her skin and face, and we decided they looked like Australian Aboriginal markings.

When the young man's mother became ill, a medicine man blessed her. As she passed, Joyce later said: "I felt an energy come into my body."

Later, the young man was playing with his son in the jungle, swinging on a long cord and jumping into the water.

Caught unawares, he was grabbed by the neck and killed by a tiger, in front of his twelve-year-old son. His soul was distraught that his son should see him die in this way.

Wisdom

Joyce brought back the wisdom of the medicine man—that the power to do whatever we want is within us. The journey also confirmed her role in this lifetime, which has subsequently expanded into other metaphysical work.

Charles

Charles came to the clinic suffering from depression and anxiety. He was a financial analyst by profession and the son of a banker. He had always been drawn to the solitary life, but had rejected religion in his teens. Not long after leaving university, he fell into a major depression, during which he began to read everything he could find on religion and spirituality. He was living a dual life—banking and finance by day and seeking spiritual wisdom and understanding at other times.

First Life

In his first past-life regression, Charles was a Jesuit monk whose mission was to serve Christ with love and compassion. He lived simply and in near poverty in an 18th-century monastery. When he returned to the present, Charles was clearly disturbed by the experience. He felt that he had avoided his feelings in the life he was leading and that he was not upholding the values of dignity, tolerance, justice, and honor that his past life had taught him.

Second Life

In his second past-life regression, Charles was a cleric at a mosque in Mecca, around 1200 AD. While defending the city against the Crusaders, he died when a sword was driven through his heart. He believed the wisdom of this life was that only through caring for and engaging with others can we find happiness. He was saddened, however, by the feeling that there were limits to what people could do to protect their friends and family.

Third Life

Charles's third regression took him to the Middle East, where he had been a male slave who was abused. This life's lesson — that when you lose faith in God, you go adrift — had a profound impact on Charles.

Wisdom

Through the three past-life regressions he underwent, Charles was able to put his present life into perspective and came to realize the source of his conflict with his family and their values. He made the decision to leave his career in business and go into teaching.

The Power Combination—Past-Life and Interlife Journeys
Dennis

Dennis, a construction worker, came into the clinic because he hadn't been able to shake the grief of losing his beloved girl friend. She had died unexpectedly two years previously and he still carried the pain. He was also hoping for clarity about a goal he had of working with underprivileged children, helping to lead them into a healthy lifestyle of exercise and nutrition.

First Life

Dennis came into this life as a Japanese pilot being given a medal of honor by the King (he said) of Japan. He felt proud but very sad and disturbed by the process. In the following scene, he was home with his beloved wife and children (his girlfriend in this lifetime) and she was crying because she didn't want him to go to war. Then he moved to the experience of guiding his squadron toward the British battleships in the ocean, and commanding the pilots to fly their planes — one by one — into the ships to destroy them. He watched as his pilots killed themselves and then completed the task by doing the same thing himself. I recognized that he was, at that time, a Kamikaze pilot.

Wisdom

All this time, Dennis was sobbing, recognizing the pain of power and leadership. And the caution needed when accepting a leadership role.

Second Life

Dennis entered the streets of Chicago in the 1930s with a machine gun under his arm, leading a group in a gang war. His gang won the fight and left a dozen men lying dead on the streets. He felt jubilant and powerful. He went home to his wife and children, but felt nothing for them—to him they were more of a nuisance than anything.

The next scene, once again on the streets of Chicago, involved a battle with the police. This time, Dennis and his gang lost the fight. They were all killed, leaving Dennis in shock. Although still in hypnosis, the conscious part of him found it hard to believe he could have behaved that way.

Wisdom
Dennis learned to be aware of the power of leadership, and the dangers inherent in leadership without an understanding of cause and effect.

The Interlife
Dennis followed up this profound past-life-regression journey with a three-hour Interlife session. He slipped into hypnosis easily and entered through the gates of light, where he was met by "the most beautiful being of light," who led him to a garden of healing—a beautiful place filled with golden sunshine, everything shimmering with light. He was asked to lie down on the grass and inhale the fragrance of the flowers surrounding him.

Dennis became aware of others in this garden and discovered that everyone he had led to their death was there—the Japanese pilots and the Chicago gang. All were lying in the shimmering grass. Beings of light moved among them, laying on hands in circles of light above each of the men. All these souls were being healed in this place. Tears of joy spilled down his face as he recognized the men and how he and they were being filled with love, healing, and light.

He resisted moving on in the journey for some time, until his guide told him that he would be taken to the place of the soul circle. He arrived there and found himself surrounded by a large group of noisy, happy, laughing child-souls who were very glad to see him. He stayed there for a while, feeling the love and joy. Then he noticed a soul waiting for him just beyond the circle. He felt the presence of his girlfriend and the love she was sending him. I suggested that, if he chose to, he could ask her why she had left him in this lifetime. She told him it was so that he could learn forgiveness—for himself and others—and so that he could discover his soul light and use that knowledge for his future.

This was so profound an experience for Dennis that he didn't want to go further with the Interlife journey (by this time we were at the two-and-a-half-hour mark!). When he came out of hypnosis, he knew that he had all the answers he needed to move forward with his plan for children, out of integrity and love—not power—and that he needed to leave the pain and anger of his early childhood behind, where it belonged.

Joy in Life

Stretch your mind and fly.

—African Proverb

Adele

First Life

Adele, a successful real estate agent, wanted to explore why she always felt poor and was concerned about money, even though she didn't need to be.

Slipping easily into the past life, Adele found herself in a very simple home at mealtime, eating salty oatmeal from a wooden bowl with two other children—a younger girl with blonde hair and a boy. Her father, she knew, worked in the fields and would be home later.

Suddenly, they were leaving in a hurry and Adele knew her mother was worried. It was dark and they were running away from a fire. The fields were on fire and people were gathering by a river, trying to get across. Everyone managed to get away from the fire, but their homes were destroyed.

Later, Adele found herself on a street in a town. She was about twenty years old and had a child with her; they were going somewhere. She was holding the child's hand and they were walking. The streets and buildings were made of stone. She was shopping and had coins with which to buy things. It was her daughter's birthday and they were celebrating.

She arrived home after a long walk over a bridge just outside of town. There were small cottages surrounded by rolling hills. Her husband, John, was tall, with a beard, and his clothes were dirty. He worked very hard. They prayed to God for work and food, but there were also happy times, with celebrations and festivals. John reminded her of her ex-husband in her present life who had left her and moved back to Europe to be with his family.

Then it was winter, cold, with snow, but the fire kept them warm. Adele was sewing, making clothes by candlelight. She was pregnant and felt heavy. At the birth, there were women around her, helping. The baby was a boy. He was fine, but she was very tired and died soon after.

Wisdom

Adele believed the joy of this life was in her family and that, although they were poor and didn't have much, they were happy. When she left the clinic, she felt her future held possibilities for loving again and being in a happy and loving relationship.

Joy in Simplicity

Success is not fame or money or the power to bewitch. It is to have created something valuable from your own individuality and skill—a garden, an embroidery, a painting, a cake, a life.

—CHARLOTTE GRAY

Ricardo

First Life

Ricardo was a librarian who admitted that he was a bit of a recluse. Although happy on his own, he wondered why he didn't feel the need to have a wife and family.

Ricardo's regression began with him as a woman in suede moccasins with black braids. She slept under the stars at night, away from some of the group. At one point, there was a ceremony in which feathered headdresses were worn, and there was much dancing as a form of release. Ricardo did not participate; he watched. The woman's role in the group was to take care of children, to keep them out of danger, and to mend their clothes.

The group or tribe the woman belonged to did not live in teepees. They were nomadic and moved with the seasons, following the food. Her life was simple and pre-ordained. She was peaceful with the order of things and expected no more.

Wisdom

For Ricardo, the joy and wisdom in this life came from its simplicity—from living with nature and raising children. It helped him understand why, in his present life, he has always needed to travel and feels like an outsider. We discussed what possibilities might emerge from this understanding, and he left the clinic more open to a different future for himself.

Joy in Personal Happiness

When one door is closed, another is sure to open. That is the thought that sustains me.

—HELEN KELLER

Bob

Third Life

Bob had been to the clinic before for past-life regressions and each time he left with some tools to enable him to improve his current life. This time, he wanted to explore his interest in the military—he collected toy soldiers and set them up in historic battle formations.

Slipping easily into past life, Bob became a fifteen-year-old male living outside a small town near a rain forest. His home was very plain, made of mud-brick walls. He walked for transportation because there was no other way. He lived with his parents and a sister.

Bob's father worked with stone as a carver and created monuments. But Bob wanted to be a warrior and write poetry that told of sacrifice and honor. He eventually joined a band of warriors that raided other settlements for food and wives. When they were successful, Bob was the storyteller for the group. Bob left this life when he was killed during a bloody battle.

Wisdom

Bob believed he got the most joy in this life from the telling of the story, but came to understand that there is no romance in violence. He was very young and embraced what was beautiful in life, but learned that the passions of the heart should be tempered by the mind—that no cause is so great that it supersedes personal happiness.

Bob left the clinic still wondering why he played with toy soldiers, but now understood that it was his form of artistic self-expression—making historic battle formations. "Hey," he said, "some guys play with trains. I play with toy soliders!"

Responsibility

Live so that thou mayest desire to live again—that is thy duty—for in any case thou wilt live again!
—FRIEDRICH NIETZSCHE

Norah

Norah was a young woman who had never felt connected to her mother or her siblings. She was a tomboy during her childhood and became a firefighter as an adult. She felt so different and unconnected from her family that she wondered if, in fact, she had been adopted.

First Life

In her first past-life regression, Norah was a Native American woman with a husband and children. When her husband died in battle, she was forced to live independently and ultimately died alone, but at peace. On returning to the present, she questioned whether she had dealt well with the grief of feeling unloved by her family in her current life.

Second Life

In her second past-life journey, Nora was a woman who joined a group in revolt against the French king; she was stabbed to death during a street fight. She left the life wondering if she could have been more courageous.

Third Life

In her third past life, Nora was a medicine man in Africa who felt responsible when his patient died. He was sent away by his tribe—banished as a failure—and felt that he had been treated unjustly. He was angry and bitter.

Wisdom

Norah carries a huge burden of responsibility in her present life. By choosing to be a firefighter, she realized that she is quite possibly attempting to assuage the feelings of guilt and inadequacy she has brought forward from these past lives. When she left the clinic, she had decided to do more work to release this guilt and her feelings of not being good enough.

Be True to Yourself

Few are those who see with their own eyes and feel with their own hearts.

— ALBERT EINSTEIN

Fiona

Fiona is a homeopathic doctor who always felt a strong affinity to Atlantis and all things Asian and Oriental. She came in for past-life regression to see if it could help some of her patients with their issues, but she wanted to try it first.

First Life

In her first life, Fiona was a female in Switzerland in 1546, in love with a man who reminded her of her current husband. She married him, but he soon became irritating and demanding. She was disappointed and heartbroken—this was not what she had expected. She left him and lived the next part of her life alone and feeling lonely. She felt free only when he died.

Wisdom

Fiona believes the lesson of this life is to learn to express her true feelings and to trust herself.

Second Life

In her second life, Fiona was a young male philosophy teacher in Greece in 560 BCE. He traveled from town to town teaching. As he grew older, he became quite well known. He was sad, however, because people came to him for wisdom, but didn't follow his advice.

Wisdom

The wisdom that came from this life, according to Fiona, is to follow your own path and know yourself.

Third Life

In her third life, Fiona found herself in a temple in Atlantis. Her work was to instruct women to find their highest selves. She believed she was a high priestess—someone with strong values who was respected and who never wavered in her responsibility.

Wisdom

The wisdom of this life told Fiona to believe in the power of women and their understanding. She left the clinic more sure of the path and career she had chosen and wanting to come back for more!

Courage

Whatever you can do, or dream you can do, begin it.
Boldness has genius, power, and magic in it. Begin it now.
— GOETHE

Mark

Mark was a businessman and entrepreneur who wanted to understand where his addiction to risk came from.

First Life

In his first regression, Mark was a teenage male on a slave ship, unloading dead bodies. He was in England, probably around 1780. At some point, he found himself in port, a place with palm trees and people wearing sarongs. He met a woman with whom he fell in love, but he had to leave her for a while to return to the slave ship. Eventually, he went back to her and stayed for a month. Over time, they had a daughter and other children, and lived a happy, easy life—until his eldest son was killed in an accident. He felt the pain of losing a loved one for the first time.

Wisdom

Mark believed that the wisdom of this life was: Don't be afraid to give.

Second Life

In his second past-life regression, Mark was a female in her thirties in the early 1900s, probably in America. She was a writer with no job, who wrote stories she couldn't sell. She finally decided to cut her hair, wear a man's suit, and pretend to be a man. A publisher eventually bought one of her stories. She eventually met a man, who became her friend, then her lover, and then her husband.

Wisdom

This life's lesson, according to Mark, is to have courage and tenacity: never give up.

Consider This

- What has your current life given you that, when you look back, gives you a feeling of "Aha"?

- If you draw your current life as a road map, can you see the forks in the road where you made choices?

- Can you see any patterns or consistencies here?

◆

There is no end! One life follows another as sunrise follows moonset. We are part of the rhythm of all there is—like the ebb and flow of the tides, the waxing and waning of the moon, the change of the seasons. Our breath carries the rhythm of life for us on this planet today. Connecting us to all there is, through time and space.

I wish for you joy and peace in each moment, and the recognition and understanding that, to choose each moment how we are, makes us who we are in this current lifetime.

Enjoy your moments in peace, love, and recognition of your connection to the light.

Namaste.

Bibliography and Additional Resources

Interlife

There is a noble and exciting heritage and ongoing research of writing, recording, and researching the Interlife, or Bardo. Here are some of the better-known names in that research community whose work is worth exploring.

Buckman, Robert. *Human Wildlife: The Life that Lives on Us.* Johns Hopkins University Press, 2003.

Cannon, Dolores. *Between Death and Life, Conversations with a Spirit.* Huntsville, AR: Ozark Mountain Publishing, Inc., 1995.

———. *Jesus and the Essenes.* Huntsville, AR: Ozark Mountain Publishers, New edition, 1999.

———. *Legacy from the Stars.* Huntsville, AR: Ozark Mountain Publishing, 1996.

Dalai Lama, Jeffrey Hopkins, and Tenzin Gyatso. *The Meaning of Life.* Somerville, MA: Wisdom Publications, Revised edition, 2000.

Denning, Hazel M. *True Hauntings: Spirits with a Purpose*. St. Paul, MN: Llewellyn Publications, 1996.

———. *Life Without Guilt: Healing Through Past Life Regression*. St. Paul, MN: Llewellyn Publications, 1998.

Fremantle, Francesca and Chögyam Trungpa, trans. *The Tibetan Book of the Dead*. Boston, MA: Shambhala Publications Inc., 1975.

Gonzáles-Wippler, Migene. *What Happens After Death: Scientific and Personal Evidence for Survival*. St. Paul, MN: Llewellyn Publications, 1997.

Hallett, Elisabeth. *Soul Trek: Meeting Our Children on the Way to Birth*. Hamilton, MT: Light Hearts Publishing, 1995.

Iverson, Jeffrey. *In Search of the Dead: A Scientific Investigation of Evidence for Life After Death*. BCA (1993) and BBC TV series.

Kelleher, Susan. *Spirit Dogs: Life Between Lives*. Silverthorne, CO: Owl of Athene Press, 2005.

Lucas, Winafred Blake. *Regression Therapy: A Handbook for Professionals*, Volume 2. Crest Park, CA: Deep Forest Press, 1993.

McKibbin, Gates. *The Life of the Soul: The Path of Spirit in Your Lifetimes*. Healdsburg, CA: Field Flowers, Inc., 1999.

Newton, Michael. *Journey of Souls: Case Studies of Life Between Lives*. St. Paul, MN: Llewellyn Publications; 1994.

———. *Memories of the Afterlife: Life Between Lives, Stories of Personal Transformation*. St. Paul, MN: Llewellyn Publications; 1st edition, 2009.

Sinnett, A. P. *Life Between Lives*. Whitefish, MT: Kessinger Publishing, 2005.

Stevenson, Ian. *Where Reincarnation and Biology Intersect.* Westport, CT: Praeger Publishers, 1997.

Whitton, Joel L. and Joe Fisher. *Life Between Life: Scientific Explorations into the Void Separating One Incarnation from the Next.* New York: Warner Books, 1986.

Woolger, Roger J. *Healing Your Past Lives: Exploring the Many Lives of the Soul.* Boulder, CO: Sounds True Inc., U.S., Har/Com edition, 2004.

Past Lives

The research and recording of past lives has been extensive. These further readings I suggest are just a beginning. Keep exploring and reading other experiences, but always with discernment—remembering, as you did in this book, that it is only one person's point of view. All are worth considering, however, and perhaps worthy of taking into your own experience and knowledge bank.

Andrews, Ted. *How to Uncover Your Past Lives.* St. Paul, MN: Llewellyn Publications, 1997.

Baldwin, William J. and Edith Fiore. *Spirit Releasement Therapy: A Technique Manual.* Terra Alta, WV: Headline Books, 1992.

Bolduc, Henry Leo. *The Journey Within: Past-Life Regression and Channeling.* Independence, VA: Adventures into Time Publishers, 1988.

———. *Life Patterns: Soul Lessons and Forgiveness.* Independence, VA: Adventures into Time Publishers, 1994.

Bowman, Carol. *Children's Past Lives: How Past Life Memories Affect Your Child*. New York: Bantam Books, 1997.

Brennan, J. H. *The Reincarnation Workbook: A Complete Course in Recalling Past Lives*. Wellingborough, UK: Aquarian Press, 1989.

Browne, Sylvia. *Life on the Other Side: A Psychic's Tour of the Afterlife*. New York: Signet, 2000.

———. *The Other Side and Back: A Psychic's Guide to Our World and Beyond*. New York: Signet, 2000.

———. *Past Lives, Future Healing: A Psychic Reveals the Secrets to Good Health and Good Relationships*. New York: Dutton, 2001.

Chopra, Deepak. *How To Know God: The Soul's Journey into the Mystery of Mysteries*. New York: Harmony Books, 2000.

Cranston, Sylvia and Carey Williams. *Reincarnation: A New Horizon in Science, Religion, and Society*. New York: Julian Press, 1984.

Evans-Wentz, W. Y. *The Tibetan Book of the Dead*. New York: Oxford University Press, 1960.

Fiore, Edith. *You Have Been Here Before: A Psychologist Looks at Past Lives*. New York: Ballantine Books, 1986.

Gabriel, Michael and Marie Gabriel. *Remembering your Life Before Birth: How Your Womb Memories Shaped Your Life and How to Heal Them*. Santa Rosa, CA: Aslan Publishing, 1995.

Gershom, Rabbi Yonassan. *Beyond the Ashes: Cases of Reincarnation from the Holocaust*. Virginia Beach, VA: A.R.E. Press, 1992.

Goldberg, Bruce. *Past Lives, Future Lives*. New York: Ballantine Books, 1988.

Iverson, Jeffrey. *In Search of the Dead: A Scientific Investigation of Evidence for Life after Death*. London: Penguin Group and BBC Enterprises, 1992.

Lucas, Winafred Blake. *Regression Therapy: A Handbook for Professionals*, Volumes I and II. Crest Park, CA: Deep Forest Press, 1996.

Oliver, Mary. "The Journey," in *Dreamwork*. New York: Atlantic Monthly Press, 1986.

Shroder, Thomas. *Old Souls: Compelling Evidence from Children Who Remember Past Lives*. New York: Simon and Schuster, 2001.

Stearn, Jess. *Edgar Cayce: The Sleeping Prophet*. New York: Bantam Books, 1967.

Steiger, Brad. *You Will Live Again: Dramatic Case Histories of Reincarnation*. Nevada City, CA: Blue Dolphin Publishing, 1996.

Stevenson, Ian. *Children Who Remember Previous Lives: A Question of Reincarnation*. Jefferson, NC: McFarland and Co., 2000.

TenDam, Hans. *Exploring Reincarnation: The Classic Guide to the Evidence for Past-Life Experiences*. London: Arkana, 1990.

Thomas, Hanna. *Explorers of Humankind*. San Francisco: Harper and Row, 1979.

Weiss, Brian. *Many Lives, Many Masters*. New York: Fireside, 1988.

———. *Through Time into Healing: Discovering the Power of Regression Therapy to Erase Trauma and Transform Mind, Body, and Relationships*. New York: Fireside, 1993.

Whitton, Joel L. and Joe Fisher. *Life Between Life: Scientific Explorations into the Void Separating One Incarnation from the Next.* New York: Warner Books, 1986.

Woolger, Roger J. *Other Lives, Other Selves: A Jungian Psychotherapist Discovers Past Lives.* New York: Bantam, 1988.

Additional Reading

As with all subjects, an understanding of past-life regression journeys and the Interlife experience needs to be seen in a larger context if it is to be meaningful. These suggested readings give a wider perspective in which to place your views and experiences of life and Interlife travels.

Bede, the Honorable. *History of the English Church and People.* New York: Penguin Classics, 1955.

Coelho, Paolo. *The Alchemist.* San Francisco: HarperOne, 2006.

Dante. *The Inferno*, trans. Allen Mandelbaum. New York: Bantam Classics, 1982.

de Mello, Anthony. "Awareness: The Perils and Opportunities of Reality," in *The Illusion of Rewards*, ed. J. Francis Stroud. New York: Doubleday, 1992.

Emoto, Masaru. *The Hidden Messages in Water.* New York: Atria, 2001.

Harderwijk, Rudy. "Buddhist Karma," *A View on Buddhism. www.buddhism.kalachakranet.org/karma.html.* 8 November 2007.

Henderson, Ian Victor. *Parables of Life: An Awakening Journey. http://www.scribd.com/doc/59121029/Parables-of-Life.*

Jacobson, Leonard. *Journey into Now: Clear Guidance on the Path of Spiritual Awakening*. La Selva Beach, CA: Conscious Living Publications, 2007.

Jenkins, Palden. "Psychic Abortions" (1999). *www.palden.co.uk/palden/p4-childbirth.html*.

Keller, Helen and Anne Sullivan. *The Story of My Life*. New York: Doubleday, 1938.

Lawton, Ian. *The Book of the Soul: Rational Spirituality for the Twenty-first Century*. Rational Spirituality Press, 2004; on the web at *www.awakening-spirits.net/book.htm*.

McGill, Ormond. *Grieve No More, Beloved: The Book of Delight*. Wales, UK: Crown House Publishing Limited, 2003.

McLean, Richard. *Zen Fables for Today*. New York: Avon Books, 1998.

Myss, Caroline. *Anatomy of the Spirit: The Seven Stages of Power and Healing*. New York: Three Rivers Press, 1996.

Sigmund, Stephen. *Organic Gardening, Vol 31*. New York: Rodale, 1984.

Spitz, Rabbi Elie Kaplan. *Does the Soul Survive? A Jewish Journey to Belief in Afterlife, Past Lives and Living with Purpose*. Woodstock, VT: Jewish Lights Publishing, 2000.

Staume, David. *The Beginner's Guide for the Recently Deceased: A comprehensive travel guide to the only inevitable destination*. St. Paul, MN: Llewellyn Publications, 2004.

Thurman, Robert A. F., trans. *The Tibetan Book of the Dead*. New York: Bantam Books, 1994.

Walsch, Neale Donald. *The Little Soul and the Sun: A Children's Parable Adapted from Conversations With God*. Newburyport, MA: Hampton Roads Pub. Co., 1998.

Williamson, Marianne. *A Return to Love*. New York: Harper
Paperbacks, 1996.

Organizations

American Society of Psychical Research
www.aspr.com

Association for Research and Enlightenment (ARE), the
Edgar Cayce Foundation
www.are-cayce.com

Children's Past Lives Research Center
www.childpastlives.org

David Bennett
Dharma-Talks.com

International Association of Research and Regression
Therapies (IARRT)
www.iarrt.org

International Board of Regression Therapies (IBRT)
www.ibrt.org

Michael Newton and the Newton Institute for Life Between
Lives Hypnotherapy
www.spiritualregression.org

Princeton Engineering Anomalies Research (PEAR)
www.princeton.edu/~pear/

Society for Psychical Research
anomalyinfo.com

About the Author

 Dr. Georgina Cannon is an award-winning board certified hypnotherapist and the founder of the Toronto-based Ontario Hypnosis Centre, the Canada's leading hypnosis training facility and hypnotherapy clinic. She hosts the Shirley MacLaine website chat room monthly talking about hypnosis and past and interlife regression. She leads workshops in Europe, the Middle East and the U.S., and Canada.

In 2003, the CBC produced a three part series on Past Life Regression filmed in her clinic with Dr. Cannon as the key player in the program. This program has been repeated both in Canada and internationally on the History and Discovery channels. Dr. Cannon is a regular public speaker and is a lecturer at the University of Toronto's School of Social Work teaching Practical Hypnosis for Social Workers. She has written and produced 24 self-hypnosis compact discs. She lives in Toronto. Visit her online at *www.georginacannon.com*.

To Our Readers